A Letter to My Congregation

An evangelical pastor's path to
embracing people who are gay, lesbian
and transgender in the company of Jesus

Ken Wilson

Read The Spirit Books

an imprint of
David Crumm Media, LLC
Canton, Michigan

For more information and further discussion, visit
www.ALetterToMyCongregation.com

Cover art and design by
Rick Nease
www.RickNeaseArt.com

Published By
Read The Spirit Books
an imprint of
David Crumm Media, LLC
42015 Ford Rd., Suite 234
Canton, Michigan, USA

For information about customized editions, bulk purchases
or permissions, contact David Crumm Media, LLC at info@
DavidCrummMedia.com

Contents

Dedication

In loving memory of Nancy.
In gratitude for Dr. Sam Tickle.
In hope of finding Andrew.

Consequently, you are no longer foreigners and strangers, but fellow citizens with God's people, and you belong to his household, built on the foundation of the apostles and prophets with Christ Jesus himself as the cornerstone. The whole building is joined together in him, and it grows to become a temple that is dedicated to the Lord. And in him you too are being built together into a dwelling in which God dwells by his Spirit.

(Ephesians 2: 19-22)

Foreword

By Dr. David P. Gushee

I SPENT MUCH of 2013 reading the collected works of the great German theologian Dietrich Bonhoeffer, who was executed by the Nazis in April 1945, just three weeks before Adolf Hitler killed himself in a Berlin bunker. Bonhoeffer was a genius, and as a young prodigy with two dissertations already under his belt by the age of 24 was slated for a brilliant career in the elite German university world. But his emergence occurred concurrently with Hitler's emergence. Bonhoeffer's steadfast resistance to the Nazi regime and the Nazi seduction of the churches eventually cost him everything: reputation, opportunity, career, freedom, and finally his life.

In a December 1942 letter to his co-conspirators against the Nazi regime, most of them also drawn from elite ranks of German society, Bonhoeffer reflected on the costs that he and many others had already paid. Already banned from publishing, preaching, or teaching in Germany, Bonhoeffer wrote:

There remains an experience of incomparable value.
We have for once learnt to see the great events of
world history from below, from the perspective of
the outcast, the suspects, the maltreated, the pow-
erless, the oppressed, the reviled—in short, from
the perspective of those who suffer.
(from Letters and Papers from Prison)

In many contemporary evangelical churches, gays
and lesbians are the premier outcast group. They are the
maltreated, the powerless, the oppressed, and the reviled.
And they have suffered much. They have suffered at the
hands of the church, especially its preachers and pastors;
they have suffered at the hands of millions of Christians who
have believed the rejection and exclusion of gays to be an
appropriate application of the Christian faith.

The maltreatment of gays and lesbians in Christianity has
been the result of a particular reading of particular biblical
passages that has calcified into a hardened tradition over the
course of church history. This tradition has created a Christian
moral world in which gays and lesbians can find no place
other than as the condemned. Sometimes that condemnation
has been physically or verbally violent; more recently, in
part due to gains by gay activists, it has retreated toward a
more mild but still unsatisfactory "love the sinner, hate the
sin" motif, as Ken Wilson notes in this important book. But
even this modification has not been enough to spare gays and
lesbians the constant experience of rejection and exclusion at
the hands of Christians, in families, schools, and churches.

By asking first his Vineyard Church movement, and now
through this book the wider Christian world, to reconsider its
posture toward gays and lesbians, Wilson has already tasted
"the perspective of the outcast, the suspects, the maltreated,
the powerless, the oppressed, the reviled." By even suggesting
that the traditional interpretation of biblical passages might
need to be reconsidered, and that the sexual morality of

committed gay relationships might be viewed as a "disputable matter" of opinion (Romans 14) rather than settled and non-negotiable dogma, Wilson has moved from the religious "above" to the religious "below." He has tasted that "experience of incomparable value ... the perspective of those who suffer." By standing in pastoral solidarity with gays, his reputation has been tarnished. And that will only deepen after this brilliant book is read across the land in days to come.

I believe that this is a breakthrough work coming from the heart of evangelical Christianity and offered into the heart of evangelical Christianity. It is unlike other books that demand revision of traditional Christian sexual ethics but do so primarily by rejecting the authority of the Bible. That is not how evangelicals think, and it is not what Wilson does here. Instead Wilson shows how God has led him on a journey toward a rethinking of what the fully authoritative and inspired Bible ought to be taken to mean in the life of the church today.

There is so much to love here: the way Ken so thoughtfully leads the reader on the journey with him; the skillful biblical/scholarly digging that actually reveals how careless much "biblical scholarship" is on this matter; the deeply respectful treatment of differences; and the pastoral heartbeat that pulses through the whole book. Perhaps most surprising and moving is Ken's emphasis on God's Spirit at work in his own life and ministry. Ken reports experiences with God's Spirit here that will seem alien to those of us whose faith is not quite as supernatural as in his own tradition. In a sense this book is a gift from the more Spirit-attuned part of the evangelical world to the rest of us.

How do ancient religious communities change their minds? How do traditional scriptural interpretations that have hardened into dogma get broken open for fresh thinking? A key role is played by courageous religious leaders who become convinced that change is needed. Only such leaders have the experience, skill, and authority to make a faith community consider the possibility of changing its mind. The problem is that such leaders generally have too much at stake in the religious status quo to be able to see the need for a change; or if they do see such a need, they risk too much to be willing to pay the price to initiate it, and so they remain silent.

You may not find yourself persuaded by Wilson's argument in *Letter to My Congregation*. But I challenge you to enter with him on the journey he describes in this book. Read it from the first page to the last page. Read it prayerfully. See what God wants to say to you through the reflections of this conscientious and courageous pastor.

David P. Gushee is the Distinguished University Professor of Christian Ethics and Director of the Center for Theology and Public Life at Mercer University. An active Baptist, Professor Gushee was the principal drafter of both the Evangelical Climate Initiative (2006) and the Evangelical Declaration against Torture (2007), both of which changed the conversation in church and society about their respective issues. His many books include A New Evangelical Manifesto: A Kingdom Vision for the Common Good; The Sacredness of Human Life: Why an Ancient Biblical Vision is Key to the World's Future; and Evangelical Peacemakers: Gospel Engagement in a War-Torn World.

Preface

By Dr. Tanya Luhrmann

EVANGELICALS ARE POORLY understood by people
like myself who might be described as "secular." My book
When God Talks Back, reporting on many years of research,
shows that evangelical Christians have to work hard to
experience God and that the willingness to do this work is a
major feature of evangelical Christianity in the 21st century.
This experiential dimension of faith means that evangelicals
are not simply receiving religious dogma and playing it out
(though there is plenty of that). They are also on a journey that
sometimes leads to surprising places.

For most evangelical Christians, prayer is not the rote
recitation of scripted words. Prayer is a conversation with
God. People talk to God, usually in their minds, and they
seek to listen to what God might be saying to them in return
by seeking to discern God's voice among the tumult of their
own thoughts and sensations. This is an old, old practice that
we sometimes associate with Ignatius Loyola, but has even
deeper roots among the Church fathers. Evangelicals assume

that God is always talking but that the voice is muffled by our own human wants and fears, and that it takes courage and honesty to listen well. What struck me, in my own research, was how thoughtful people were in their own practices of discernment, and how the practice of careful listening could impact someone. In *A Letter to My Congregation* we see an evangelical pastor wrestling with the traditional exclusionary approach to people who are gay and lesbian, wrestling with his understanding of God and Scripture, wrestling with his experience as a pastor, and changing his mind, which is exactly what prayer does.

This is a remarkable and timely book. I say this not as an advocate or stakeholder, but as a scholar: a professional observer of evangelical Christianity. And it is clear to an observer like me that evangelical Christianity is at a crossroad. The question of whether gay Christians should be married within the church is a symptom of the problem, not the problem itself. That problem is the broad and widening gap between evangelical Christianity and its young.

The data seem clear that young adults brought up in the evangelical church are substantially more liberal than their parents on a range of social issues. There is a panicked claim that only a tiny percentage of today's teenagers will be Bible-believing adults. That's probably exaggerated. There are also loud counter-arguments that these fears are entirely ungrounded. But the bulk of the evidence suggests that young evangelicals are indeed more progressive than their seniors, and that support for gay marriage is only the most visible of their concerns (environmental care and poverty are others; they seem also to be more willing to treat abortion as a personal choice).

Some observers (myself among them) think that this waning of support for the traditional political stances of the evangelical right may be in part responsible for the rising number of "nones," or those who say that they are not affiliated to any church. The General Social Survey found that in 2012, 20 percent of the American population described themselves as unaffiliated to any church, a five point increase since 2007. Most of those people aren't atheists or even agnostics (again, we know this by the numbers, these are from the Pew Research Center). They just don't have a church with which they want to be identified.

It seems time for the church to determine whether the political commitments that may be making these young people hesitate are not, in fact, founded on scriptural authority but are the product of something else—local politics, perhaps, or the tidal flow of middle class opinion in the 1970s and '80s.

That is what Ken Wilson is asking his readers to consider. He writes that he began his Christian journey at a time when many assumed that to be a Christian, one had to hold a series of attitudes about sexuality because that's what the Bible said. Now decades later, he has begun to wonder whether some of these attitudes were in fact the product of his time, and not truth embedded in the scriptures. He is still a deeply committed Bible-believing Christian. But he has prayed with depth and feeling, and he has come to conclusions different from those he once held. He is asking his readers to read the Bible with him again with an open heart and to reflect anew on what it says.

The book you hold is a passionate and courageous argument. Many people will not like it. But they should read it and weigh whether it is true, because more hangs on the argument than the fate of gay marriage within evangelical Christianity. At its heart, this book asks Christians to rethink what God and scripture may be saying about what it means to be a good and decent person. The answer to that question will shape what the church becomes in twenty years.

Tanya Luhrmann is the Watkins University Professor in the Stanford Anthropology Department. Her specialty is psychological anthropology; and she served as president of the Society for Psychological Anthropology for 2008. Her research topics range from Zoroastrians to divergent models in contemporary psychiatry. Her 2012 book, When God Talks Back: Understanding the American Evangelical Relationship with God , examines how evangelical and charismatic Christians come to experience God as someone with whom they can communicate on a daily basis through prayer and visualization.

Introduction

By Phyllis Tickle

WHEN, IN THIS country, more than three or four of us
begin at any one time to talk about religion, we can almost
always count on an ensuing, and sometimes heated, difference
of opinions. Those animated exchanges spring, as a rule
anyway, from disagreements about doctrine and dogma,
creeds and postures. Rarely do they arise from any confusion
about the fact that religion really does exist among us.

Whether one is religious or not, observant or not, "spiritual
but not religious" or not, or just plain agnostic or atheistic or
not, the fact still remains that we all recognize that there is an
area of human thought and activity called "Religion" and that
it is compellingly important at a personal level for some of us
while being only tangentially present in the greater scheme
of things for some of the rest of us. But what all of us on that
spectrum also recognize is that independent of the degree—or
lack thereof—of our personal faith and commitment, religion
still exists and dwells among us as an arbitrating institution,
as an informing structure within the architecture of society;

and we accept it as such. As a part of that acceptance, we recognize as well that at the front lines of every presentation of religion, regardless of its particular confessions or creeds or theology, stand its clergy. It is primarily they through whom we, whether we be believers or not, interface with both the institution and the implications for our society of the faith and values it embodies.

Oddly enough though, unless we are Jewish, even the most faith-oriented among us in this country, tend to think of "clergy" first and foremost as that group of professionals who bury us, marry us, preach at us, counsel us and, from time to time, exercise a kind of political or moral authority for us.

The oddity in that job summary is that we ... and most particularly we Christians ... rarely think of our clergy as men and women who routinely spend agonizing hours and days and weeks pouring studiously over sacred texts in relentless, ongoing attempts to penetrate the mysteries contained there, to discover their wisdom, their instruction, their relevance, and to consider the means and repercussions of their implementation within our here and now.

And the oddity in that, of course, is that most of us, whether religious or not, have heard the term *midrash* often enough in popular movies and novels, if nowhere else, so that we know at least vaguely what it means and tries to name.

What it means and names is that informed and trained poring over Scripture ... that agonizing and intricate pursuit of nuance and particularity and then their recording so that others might see ... that endless, deep labor of awed thought followed by its careful articulation ... that weariness which comes from elusive resolution and, after that, the burden of pushing on nonetheless ... That—all of it—is *midrash*, just as surely as it is an expected and traditional rabbinic or clerical and pastoral role within Judaism.

Despite that fairly well-known fact, however, up until recently, we Christians have tended to not even recognize such arduous work as part of the contemporary clerical calling in our own communion, much less expected it, hoped for it, prayed for it. But now these times that are our times, with their swirling insecurities and burgeoning opportunities, almost compel us ... almost demand of us ... that we go looking for *midrash* ... and here, in the pages that follow, we have before us one of the most exquisite, painful, candid, brilliant pieces of contemporary Christian *midrash* that I have ever seen.

As is true with all *midrash*, some congregants—and we are all Wilson's congregants by extension—may not like the scriptural parsing and probing and proof-texting that lead to modified behavior, community change, confessional growth. None of that, though, ever unsays or disestablishes the compelling power of careful and reverent exploration of Scripture or the authority of what is discovered in that process. It certainly does not here. Nor does an ordered presentation of good *midrash* to the cleric's congregants ever quite manage to mask the agony or self-shredding of the journey that has been made for us. It certainly does not here, and I am grateful. Pray God, you will be too.

Phyllis Tickle is a scholar of religion, a journalist, an author of 36 books and is widely regarded as a leading American expert on religious publishing. An active member of the Episcopal Church, she speaks widely at universities and professional conferences and often is interviewed in prominent news media, including TIME magazine, the New York Times, USA Today, PBS, CNN and the BBC.

CHAPTER 1

A Fleeting Unease, Readily Dismissed

YOU'LL FORGIVE ME, I hope, if I don't make a beeline to the point.

The fact is, I'm opening a can of worms and they want to come out in a clump, rather than Worm One, followed by Worm Two, and so on.

In other words, I'm asking for some space to say what I want to say, how I want to say it. Have a little pity on your pastor. How dicey it can be to speak about things having to do with God, Scripture, reason, experience, tradition, culture and controversy. And people. And sex. I hope you don't mind if I meander a bit, especially at first.

Here's how it started for me: as a fleeting unease just below the diaphragm, readily dismissed. But it returned with increasing frequency, and then settled insistently, knot-like.

The conscience is a communal organ—a way of *knowing* that we do *with* others formed always in reference to others. The members of a congregation have a commonly held conscience on many, but not all, matters. A pastor stands at the crossroads of a congregation's conflicted conscience. It's a congested intersection, this place. Standing in the middle of it can be dizzying, frightening, awful, especially under the intense scrutiny that comes with religious controversy.

You have to keep your wits about you to discern whether the groaning in your gut echoes the groaning of the Spirit.

Questions of conscience also lie deep in the heart, where we encounter God. The Psalmist spoke from this place when he cried out, "You, you alone, are to be feared; and who may stand in your sight when once you are angry?" (Psalm 76:7) This cry is out of step with our times, but not out of step with our hearts. In the deepest, most central place of our being, we don't want to cross God and our not wanting to is the beginning of wisdom.

Oscar Wilde said, "Morality, like art, means drawing a line somewhere." If the world is to become a work of art, it will require the drawing of some lines.

Mine will become plain soon enough, as I seek to respond to the question facing pastors across the United States at this time: "Where do you draw the line on the gay issue?"

Strangely, very few of you have actually asked me this question directly. Congregations learn to read their pastors. And many of you sense that I've been wrestling with this one for a long time. You've heard sermons that indicate a certain lean away from the traditional consensus, perhaps. I suspect that some of you haven't asked me where I draw the line because you haven't wanted to put me on the spot. Others haven't wanted to situate me, your pastor, on what you may regard as the wrong side of an important moral issue. Or you may just be nervous for me, for us. In any case, I want to say: thank you.

It's a sign of the times that I don't feel the need to write such a letter on a range of moral concerns that affect many more of us than this one. I've *never* been asked where I draw the line on greed, even though most of us use considerably more than our fair share of limited natural resources (which might be a fair definition of greed, especially if the poor in the developing world have anything to say about it).

Somehow, at least within the broader Christian landscape, one issue has become arguably *the* defining question of biblical orthodoxy: "Where do you draw the line on the gay issue?"

When the question is asked, a lot seems to be at stake. Frequently it comes by e-mail from someone thinking about attending our church for the first time. Before bothering, she or he wants to know where we stand on this issue.

The questioners may be gay themselves. More likely, they have loved ones who are gay and have no intention of seeking God where they will be encouraged to "hate the sin" of their loved one. As if loving our loved ones isn't complicated enough.

There was a time when I answered a question on "the gay issue" by rehearsing the consensus position of Christendom: same-sex orientation itself is not sinful but any sex with a member of the same sex is outside the boundaries of holiness. I don't think I *appreciated* what I was really saying. That is, I didn't take the full impact of my answer, or my role as a pastor, into account.

I didn't imagine myself saying to a real gay, lesbian, or transgender person, a person I knew and loved as I would want to be known and loved, "You can't be baptized, or receive communion, or become a member, or serve in this or that capacity here." For a pastor to answer a question like this without deep reflection, without a brutally honest appreciation for its impact on real people, is, I think, and I say this advisedly, cowardly. For the people most affected by a pastor's answer, all this is very serious business, very personal business, something much different than a policy rendered in the abstraction sometimes referred to as "the gay controversy."

Sometimes a Pastor Has to Pay It No Mind

So let me say it up front: I'm doing my best to pay the so-called "controversy" itself as little mind as possible. Of course, I'm aware, too keenly aware, that this is the hottest hot button of our time in society and in many churches. The fact that this is so, is a work of the devil, the Evil One, Old Scratch, the hater of God and by association, humanity. Not to put too fine a point on it. The way we find our way through this controversy matters—not just the side we land on, but how we get there.

We can land on the "right" side of a controversy and keep that personified mystery of evil, called the devil, happy. So long as we cede the territory he is trying to occupy: that this moral concern deserves our attention more than all others, that one's position on this question determines one's belonging to or leaving a faith community. When we do this—and it is standard practice in many churches today—we stigmatize an entire group of people. We're not just singling "the issue" out. We are singling people out. This pleases the hater of humanity and grieves humanity's lover.

If it weren't for the people involved, affected, touched, harmed, stigmatized by this state of affairs, I'd be tempted to cede the ground—treat this as though it *is* the moral issue of our time because the spirit of the age hovering over the church tells me it is. But I don't have the luxury, being the pastor of a local congregation.

Biblical scholars can offer their best opinions on controversial issues of the day—though the big controversies often place the scholars under institutional constraints. (The scholars think twice before offering their best opinions, if to do so might negatively affect the institutions they serve. Such constraints affect us all.) Others—experts in moral theology, denominational officials, those with a media platform in the Christian world—can weigh in. The controversy itself surely affects anyone who is gay, but those effects don't become intimately personal until a pastor in a local congregation draws a line.

That's where my own fear and trembling arises: It really does matter where *pastors* of congregations land on this one.

This, more than anything else, is my concern: the underlying assumption behind any exclusionary policy has to do with belonging. It's a little too brazen—ugly, actually—to say out loud, but the assumption is, "They (the excluded people) don't belong here." If it's not the assumption, it is the effect.

The question of belonging is *the* question addressed by the gospel. I am not willing to simply leave this question in the realm of unexamined assumptions. Because it has to do with the very *heart* of the gospel: Who belongs? And how do they belong?

"And you also are among the Gentiles who belong to Jesus Christ" (Romans 1:6).

The gospel is an exciting experiment in belonging; and belonging is the deepest ache in the human heart. You can notice it most acutely when you don't have it. The Gentiles—those outside of the covenant between God and Israel—didn't have it. And then they did, through the faithfulness of Jesus Christ.

Over four decades of pastoral ministry—I got started early—you make mistakes. But the mistakes you most regret are the ones that obscure the gospel and hurt the people you love, by saying in effect, "You do not belong," to those for whom Christ died to provide a place of belonging. I have made such mistakes in the past. I'll tell you about some, but only in an effort not to repeat them.

I've written this lengthy letter to you, my congregation, to address this matter. Others may listen in, but I'm writing to discharge my responsibility to you as best I can, fearing Him to whom I will give an account.

Normally I'd simply address this in a sermon. I've written a book-length letter instead, because the calm and careful intimacy of a letter is needed for this one. Perhaps in the context of writing and reading we can create a space removed from at least some of the anxious din that surrounds this question, whenever it is broached.

I've chosen not to call for a "town hall meeting" of the congregation to thrash this out because "the gay controversy" is now at the epicenter of a great political and cultural divide that has been growing for the past thirty years. This fact stigmatizes people. It says to them, "Dealing with you is something we're at war over. When we talk about you, we get very upset. Some of us may get up and leave." Imagine walking into a meeting knowing that people were discussing the most tender, most vulnerable aspect of your being. You would feel singled out, stigmatized.

Presently, every position one might adopt is fraught with conflict and consequences, many of which are simply—well—unthinkable, especially for pastors.

We pastors, busy with many things, revert to our default setting at such times. We ask ourselves, "What do my trusted colleagues think?" We do so hoping *they've* done the homework, the praying, the discerning, the wrestling with Scripture, the pastoral engagement with people.

I'm sad to say that when I last taught on this topic several years ago, I hadn't done my homework. I hadn't spent much time studying the pertinent texts of Scripture, engaging the questions related to their interpretation and application. I simply passed on what I had received without subjecting it to scrutiny. Even though my words had potent implications for those who live, in regard to the most vulnerable aspect of their being, under intense scrutiny.

Worse: I did so without even asking what my teaching meant for the central question addressed by the gospel, the question of belonging. I owe you all much better than that. Even if I didn't owe *you*, I owe God better than that.

I started writing this letter (can you tell I've been working on it for a while?) as a kind of self-discipline. I started writing this to get away from the clamor of conflict and controversy enough to hear my own thoughts. If we can't hear our own thoughts, how can we possibly hear God's thoughts? You'd be surprised how many books are written by those trying figure out what they think about a thing.

I intend to say what I think, feel, see, understand and wonder about this question *in the hopes of framing it differently.* Because the controversy itself, the old pre-framed debate we have inherited, keeps us from going into unexplored territory that might contain treasure not to be had elsewhere.

Christians who sense that the gay issue is going to be explored in a way that probably won't lead to the traditional conclusion assume that this project can only lead to a different conclusion by dismissing scriptural concerns. Like so many controversies of its kind, this one is super-charged because it is a proxy for other concerns, including the authority of Scripture. We clench, if we do, because Scripture means a great deal to many of us. It means a lot to me. It was in Scripture, the gospel of Matthew in particular, that Jesus of Nazareth first peeked out at me and said, "Your impressions of me are wanting. There's more to me than meets your eye." Which is to say, we become *understandably* concerned when we think the authority, value, or trustworthiness of Scripture might be at stake. In our clenching at this prospect, we exert great effort to "get it right."

But sometimes the quest for the right answer keeps us from testing a variety of good ones. [1] In search of the right answer, we assume every answer other than the one we've settled on must be wrong. Forgetting that some things have more than one good answer. I'd like to think for example, that the question, "How can I love Ken?" might have many good answers, rather than one right one.

One thing about which I can assure you up front: You'll not be getting the one right answer from me on this question. But I do hope to offer a good answer, especially surrounding the part of this question that sits squarely in my lap as a pastor.

---

1 I'm grateful to Cherith Fee Nordling for this insight, gleaned from a talk she gave at the Society of Vineyard Scholars, April 19, 2013.

But how we get to such an answer matters a great deal. Do we get there by dismissing Scripture or by a more careful reading of Scripture? Do we get there by making the gospel more palatable to those with a hunger for cheap grace or by letting the gospel be itself in our day? Do we get there by listening to other voices or by following hard after the voice of Jesus? I hope you know me well enough to know which side of those dualities I want to occupy.

Time to Move Beyond a Well-Worn Binary?

The plain fact is, I don't trust or accept the way this question has been framed by the binary choice we face in answering it, summarized by the code phrases: "open and affirming" and "love the sinner, hate the sin." I say binary because each of these answers is understood in relation to its opposite, conceived of as its evil twin. To be "open and affirming" is not to "love the sinner, hate the sin." For too long, our controversies seem to boil down to conservatives and liberals (or, if you prefer, traditionalists and progressives) talking past each other for the benefit of stirring up their loyalists, as partisans do in the primary campaigns of electoral politics. The rest of us are expected to line up with our team just as soon as they show their colors.

This doesn't invite the participation of the Holy Spirit. Controversies rarely spawn genuine conversations and hearing God is the ultimate aim of any good conversation. I haven't seen the good fruit of this approach. Instead, I see a profusion of what Paul called "the works of the flesh"—especially the angry, hostile ones: hatred, discord, fits of rage, dissensions, factions, and envy. Putting aside the merits of the answers generated by this particular framing, I'm not impressed by the process that leads to these answers.

What if there is another way to go about this? A new way, a third option so numbered not because it's the only good way in relation to these previous ways, but because we can't move past a binary without introducing at least a third option. If this third way gets us to a better fourth or fifth way, more power to it!

Could we get there, to such a good-if-not-perfect answer, by going deeper into the gospel, deeper into the love of God, deeper into the Bible, deeper into what it means to belong to God (the meaning of holiness) and deeper into the reality of a new community leaning into the New Creation? I'd like to find a way that helps us do that.

For the most part, the Bible scholars and theologians and ethicists of the church have given their answers to the questions regarding homosexuality. But I will make my contribution as a pastor of the Vineyard Church of Ann Arbor—the place of service I occupy within the larger Christian community as I write this letter.

My involvement in the evangelical movement has also affected me. It has situated me close to the center of this swirling controversy that produces so much animosity and anxiety. A little background may help.

My denomination, Vineyard, is a loose affiliation of churches that arose out of the "Jesus movement" of the 1970's—when the children of the "age of Aquarius" met the founder of Christianity, as though, with typical baby boomer hubris, for the first time. Vineyard is sometimes described as a "post-denominational" church network. It's an example of how churches organize in this era of loosening attachments to religious institutions. Yet, it is also rooted in American Evangelicalism. For many years, our National Director, Berten Waggoner, served on the Executive Board of the National Association of Evangelicals, a prominent position within modern day evangelicalism. Evangelical Christians are scattered throughout virtually every denomination. The largest Protestant denomination, the Southern Baptist Convention, is thoroughly evangelical. Together with Roman Catholics, evangelicals of many stripes constitute a formidable force in society today.

I wasn't raised evangelical and my hometown, Ann Arbor, Michigan, is far from an evangelical bastion. But my leadership activities in Vineyard (I served for seven years on its national board) combined with my national leadership activities over matters like the environment and engagement with science brought me into close proximity with American Evangelicalism. There I encountered great, alarming anxiety over issues like the ordination of women, climate change, and evolution, but none so great as the angst over homosexuality. The Religious Right, a historic political alliance between evangelicals and Roman Catholics, was first organized in opposition to the Gay Rights movement.

Anxiety resides within organizations and sub-groups within society. When you are a leader within evangelicalism, you are powerfully affected by that communal anxiety, much as an animal becomes hyper-alert when a pulse of anxiety flashes through the herd, whenever any member of the herd spots a threat. Thus do groups naturally organize around their most anxious members. [2]

When an evangelical pastor even entertains a minority perspective on a matter of such intense controversy, he or she taps into the anxiety flowing through the system. It's intense. This letter may give you a sense of how that affects people like me in this world.

A pastor is the jack of many trades, master of none. In the age of specialization this intimidates pastors. I have come to believe that we pastors can only be true to our calling when we understand it as something other than another professional specialty. We are not professionals, even those of us who are paid for our service. We are members of a body with a history that precedes the age of professionalism and specialization. Yes, we study our Bibles and if we're wise, we include the tools developed by the professional Bible scholars in our toolbox, but we do so in the context of the community whose book the

2 See *Failure of Nerve: Leadership in the Age of the Quick Fix*, by Edwin H. Friedman, Church Publishing, 2007.

Bible is. We do so as followers of Jesus who are also pastors. And if we are alert to wisdom, we understand that theology is not simply an academic discipline. It's something *all* God seekers *do*.

At least that's how I console myself when the little voice in my head says, "Who are you to take on this issue?"

For better or worse, I've served you, the members of my congregation, for almost four decades. Sometimes I see your faces from the platform and think, "Still here! What a wonder! Would I still be here, listening to me, if I could get away from myself?" The church began as a small informal group in a University of Michigan dormitory room, back when I was an undergrad, before landing in my living room. There, sitting down as I am seated here writing, I took my turn communicating the Word with a handful of people who knew each other by name and by the details of our lives. That sense of intimacy between pastor and flock has never left me. I'm relying on it now more than ever to guide me as I write.

The Unusual Space a Pastor Occupies

I intend to write with the candor of a known person, a brother, a friend. And I will invite you into the unusual place I occupy as a pastor. In the process, I hope to close the experience gap that exists between so many pastors and their congregations. Too many congregations know too little about what their pastors go through in a time of intense cultural, political, and religious polarization, when people feel more free than ever to try a new church when their old one doesn't line up. Too many congregations don't know what it's like to lead in such an environment, to be true to the pastoral calling in a society that seems to revel in forming opinions and spouting them off as a form of something very much like entertainment. Too many congregations look to their pastors for simple answers to problems that their pastors see as anything but simple. And too many pastors don't trust their congregations enough to say, "It's not that simple from my point of view and here's why." If nothing else, I hope this letter makes a small contribution to closing that gap. Even more fundamentally than dealing with the "gay issue," I want to help change the way pastors and congregations understand each other.

Many care for others as I do, pastorally. We are, after all, the flesh-and-blood body of one who is a shepherd. We care for each other as shepherds care for their sheep. We notice each other and nudge each other and try to stay together with God.

But the *occupation* of a pastor has some unusual aspects not shared by everyone.

In my occupation as a pastor, I serve as the designated leader of a church with members and ministries and by-laws. If there are exclusions to be enforced, it's up to me to enforce them. This is especially the case in my role as the senior pastor, the leader of a team of pastors.

I've noticed that many who insist on excluding this or that person for this or that reason have never actually had to exclude anyone from church. I have excluded people from church, and believe me, it's not something to take lightly.

We all want our church experience to be free of conflict. Pastors do too, but we know it's not possible. Pastors must specialize in managing church conflict.

Pastors must learn to say no. If someone wants to distribute literature at election time to tell us who God would have us vote for, I'm the one who tells them no. And then listens as they tell me what a weak-kneed leader I am for not standing up for truth. I've refused to perform weddings if I didn't think the marriage had a chance. That conversation hardly ever goes well. I've told a member or two of our prayer ministry team that they cannot pray for people in ways that I deem harmful. I've called the police to forcibly remove a disruptive person, called protective services to investigate possible child abuse. I've asked a lady who brought her tambourine to church and played it with no particular connection to what the worship team was doing to please stop, as it had become a distraction.

And here's the truly unusual part of my occupation: people ask me what the Bible or God or Jesus would have them do. They ask questions of compelling moral import regarding matters that pertain to their lives. It's not that they care so much what I think. It's that they care deeply what God thinks. And what I say often has a powerful influence on what they think God thinks.

People who have left miserable marriages come to me and ask whether they can remarry and remain faithful to God. Depressed people ask me whether they will go to hell if they kill themselves, expecting a straight answer to a question that is anything but theoretical.

And yes, I know that it's my primary job to help them read, interpret and apply the Bible themselves. It's my job to help them hear God's voice. It's not my job to be the answer man for God. But when they come to me, they often come in distress for perspective they needed yesterday, if not sooner. They come in the middle of deciding. There is no pause button to press that will allow us to appoint a commission to study the issue and report back in a year. And sometimes they are talking to me because God told them to in order to hear from him. Or so they say.

I feel at such times very much like a priest. I feel like someone who is called to face God directly, representing people, and to face people directly, representing God. The frightening thing is, as members of a "royal priesthood," we are all called to be priests—to God and to each other. Humanity is the priesthood of the earth, which is God's temple. We are called to represent each other to God and to represent God to each other.

When Luther emphasized the royal priesthood, he wasn't bidding us to thumb our noses at the Roman priesthood. He was bidding us to come and die. Because great crucifying collisions occur where priests stand before God and other human beings. Ask Aaron or Jesus.

The Protestant reformers were bidding us to read the Bible ourselves, believing that even if we didn't have the ability, we have the responsibility. Looking back over five hundred years, it was an incredibly nervy thing to assert.

Fortunately, for the really big and important things—the existence of God, the reality of sin, the love of God revealed in Jesus—the Bible speaks so clearly that you have to work hard *not* to understand what it means and how it applies. But many other things, including specific questions about how we should then live in light of these big things, require a great deal more work. They require more prayer, more loving dialogue with others, more careful reading by everyone, more arduous study regarding the meaning of ancient words first written in a cultural context far removed from our own, more deliberative, Spirit-led discernment regarding how the words apply to us today, more patient fleshing out of such discernment in a real community in real time.

Such a process is demanding, especially when the issue at hand—what does the Bible say to people who experience profound same-sex attraction—is something relatively few of us actually experience. It's easier to offer easy answers when we are not the people facing the hard questions.

Is it any wonder we shirk this call to royal priesthood? When friends come to us with their moral dilemmas we listen and we offer opinions if asked. But we rarely wrestle with God as if their dilemmas were our own. We stay out of the muddy Jabbok where Jacob wrestled with the angel of the Lord until his hip came out of its socket. God is an intimidating opponent and we only have so many hips.

We have our own moral dilemmas to tend to and we find them exhausting. We struggle with them only long enough to get some relief and then gladly let them go. We make our choices the best we can and move on. If the biblical passages on greed prick our fattened hearts, we wince as we might for a flu shot. If no one else is pressing the issue, we don't give our conscience enough time to trouble us. When we encounter "hard cases" that defy easy answers, we shrug our shoulders and say, "Wow, that's a tough one!"

I have done the same. But my occupation as a pastor forces me to shirk a little bit less than I otherwise would. My occupation as a pastor forces me to step into my calling as part of the royal priesthood whether I want to or not, to wrestle with a question as though I were the one facing it personally. Believe me, there are many times I would have shirked my priestly duty but for the fact that it was expected of me and the poor person before me had no one else to turn to.

I wonder if you know what that's like? It's not something I've talked much about. But I realize that I cannot broach the question of how I respond to people who are gay without trying to tell you what that priestly role is like. Not so that you will admire me for the arduous task of being a pastor—I assume your jobs are at least as difficult as mine, though perhaps in different ways—but so that you can join me where these great crucifying collisions occur. So we can be a better royal priesthood to God and to each other.

Am I tipping my hand? That this letter, ostensibly about "the gay issue," is really about much more than that? I hope.

Before we begin, let me assure you of my intentions (at least). I will share with you an approach that is, first of all pastoral, as if I haven't already made that clear. It is my best attempt to honor people, to honor Scripture, to honor Jesus, to honor the heart of the gospel, and to honor the very legitimate differences in conscience that we bring to this matter. I'm under no illusions here: some will agree, some will disagree with my conclusions. I don't think it's my job to convince anyone of anything. By that I mean I don't feel that I'm responsible to God to convince anyone of anything. But it is my job to give you my best, even if it's not *the* best. That includes being as candid as I can be about the process that led to this letter.

Retracing a Path of Spiritual Discernment

Much of the material here was first presented as a paper at my denomination's scholarly society. You'll notice an academic flavor in parts of the letter. You'll see me minding my p's and q's and footnoting sources, especially when I'm dealing with the biblical issues. But the letter also traces a process of spiritual and pastoral discernment.

Like judgment, discernment involves critical thinking, discrimination and choice. But discernment is the fruit of worship. It requires the employment of the senses, including prayerful reflection on feelings and the full range of capacities with which we love (heart, soul, mind and strength). [3] Jesus warned against (at least) the abuse of judgment, but urged the responsibility of discernment. "Let those who have ears, hear" and "I only do what I see the Father doing" are encouragements to embrace this responsibility. And discernment is necessary in order to respond to the singular summons of Jesus: to follow.

Especially when I presented my views in a national forum of pastoral peers, it felt like I was walking through treacherous terrain—as though through a minefield at midnight, in fact. I was dealing with this contentious issue as a pastor, but many of the people I presented the paper to didn't know me as *their* pastor. I've been working for years in my local congregation to undermine the idea that the conservative-liberal divide is reliable shorthand for "faithful to God" vs. "unfaithful to God." But this wasn't my home congregation. This was my community of congregations and the current binary held sway: "open and affirming" meant "unfaithful to God" while "love the sinner, hate the sin" meant "faithful to God", because

---

3 "I beseech you therefore, brethren, by the mercies of God, that you present your bodies a living sacrifice, holy, acceptable unto God, which is your reasonable service. And be not conformed to this world: but be transformed by the renewing of your mind, that you may prove what is that good, and acceptable, and perfect, will of God." (Romans 12: 1-2)

the former was liberal and the latter, conservative. Or that was my reading of the situation in my tribe.

Let's take a closer look at the two sides of this binary. We focus on their different practices especially with respect to affirmation and exclusion: one side affirms while the other side excludes the people who practice a certain specified set of sexual behaviors. But after a long period of wrestling, I have come to see a deeper problem. Both approaches seem based on a common assumption about what is necessary to maintain "unity in the Spirit": to have unity of the Spirit we must either affirm that all homosexual acts are definitely sinful or affirm that some require our moral approval. Either way, our unity in the Spirit hinges on a common moral judgment. Some congregations maintain unity of the Spirit by being "open and affirming" while others do the same by taking the "love the sinner, hate the sin" approach. Decide before entering and stay so long as you agree, because unity depends on how you regard this one moral question.

But I am wondering... No, I *have* wondered and now I am challenging that assumption. I am saying that the assumption doesn't sound right to me. It doesn't sound like an assumption that is required by the gospel and why should our unity in the Spirit be based on something *more* than the gospel? In fact, it seems to short circuit a path that more powerfully reveals what it means to be accepted by God because of the gospel of Jesus Christ.

So here's what you can look forward to on the way to my getting to the point. I will begin by tracing the earlier stages of a long process of spiritual discernment. I will reflect not only on my own experience but also on my understanding of the experience of those I have come to know and love who are gay, lesbian, and transgender—some within the church and many without the church. I will share reasons for thinking that the traditional approach is the cause of unnecessary harm.

Then I'll shift gears and examine three important biblical concerns along the way:

1. The prohibitive texts regarding homosexuality;
2. How an often ignored part of the New Testament can help us maintain unity of the Spirit in the face of differing views regarding gay relationships;
3. How the previous controversy over "the biblical definition of marriage" might inform this one.

I will propose a new way forward, a way that is not based on the assumption that underlies both the "open and affirming" and the "love the sinner, hate the sin" approaches. This path emphasizes acceptance over either affirmation or exclusion, in keeping with the demands of the gospel. Given the anxious climate that attends this intense controversy, the reader will want me to rush to get there. But I beg your patience (again) because how we get to the places that we are going leaves trails that we blaze in getting there. And these trails remain long after the controversy at hand has waned.

The letter ends with a section that reveals, as best I can, the spiritual experience that has driven my discernment process. Without it, this book wouldn't have happened. I'm the sort of Christian who believes we talk to God, but God also talks back. It's a messy and obviously fraught business, this. But it's the part of faith that makes pastoral ministry worthwhile. The inattention to experience, the failure to reveal it and to account for it, has frustrated me about so much that I've read on this topic. We all have experiences that shape us but often that experience—of ourselves, of others, of God—is hidden, inferring that it doesn't matter. It does.

My first pass at writing this letter came out as an argument. It came across assertive and defensive—I think because I was imagining all the objections it would engender. I was internalizing the anxiety around me and it made me combative. When I read that version, I didn't like it. It unwittingly invited the reader to regard me as the Bible expert on this topic. But I'm not a Bible expert, in the sense that I am not a Bible scholar. I am a pastor who knows, reads, studies and loves the Bible.

So I decided my being a pastor doing his best with what he has—his experience, his Bible, his God: *that's good enough.*

I went back to my original inspiration—to write a confessional piece that invites you into my experience. If this is an argument, it began as one I had with myself as my experience challenged my existing beliefs and approaches. Yeats said the arguments you have with others are rhetoric; the arguments you have with yourself are poetry. I hope there's a little poetry in my rhetoric. And whether you end up agreeing with my conclusions or not, I hope you understand, when I'm done, what it's like to be a pastor embroiled in a controversy that has the power—but only if we let it—to dull our sensitivity to the voice of conscience and to the voice of God.

CHAPTER 2

Intuitions Toward a New Way Forward

IF YOU DO something long enough, you develop intuition that feels like instinct. I have a set of pastoral instincts that have played a significant role in exploring a new way forward.

Like the instinct to look for a third path when faced with two well-worn ones that each seem inadequate for different reasons. As soon as I realized that I didn't want to choose between the "open and affirming" approach and the "love the sinner, hate the sin" one, I assumed there must be a third option. This way of avoiding the trap of an assumed binary was the originating genius of my denomination, Vineyard. We began by questioning what turned out to have been a false choice in the "charismatic wars," a sharp difference over the role of the Spirit in the church today. Some Christians, called Pentecostals or Charismatics, wanted a powerful experience of the Spirit, replete with gifts of healing, prophecy, and ecstatic worship. Other Christians viewed this with great suspicion, partly because they couldn't agree with the understanding of Scripture that seemed attached to these practices. Yet, the Scripture bore witness to something other than the rationalistic faith they were practicing. My denomination came into existence when some of the Christians in this latter group began to ask, "How do we get the Pentecostal experience of the Spirit, without adopting the whole Pentecostal package?" (This is a longer story that I've written about elsewhere.) [4]

The emerging "gay wars" felt eerily similar. Must I choose between two options that seemed inadequate? Of course not! Look for a third way, it must be there somewhere.

Dissatisfied with the Available Options

My discomfort with the "open and affirming" position—other than the fact that adopting it would brand me as a heretic for life among my evangelical colleagues, whose opinion of me means a great deal to me, but that's a side issue—boiled down to a couple of things. Close to home, I didn't think it honored choices that dear friends had made to live celibate or to marry despite same-sex attraction. I know people who have experienced strong same-sex attraction but who view sexual orientation as changeable, fluid, open to further influence that changes their experience. From what I know, most "open and affirming" churches would dismiss their experience. But I know some of these people *well* and trust them to be the arbiters and interpreters of their own experience. How could I trust an approach that dismissed their experience as unenlightened when they understood it otherwise?

Furthermore, I didn't think that the "open and affirming" position was developed with a high enough regard for Scripture. Admittedly, this was based on a narrow range of experience and no doubt involves some bias on my part. So, let me say where I think that bias comes from. I was (and still am, proudly) a Jesus freak, circa 1971. The Jesus movement didn't follow the trajectory of the liberal Protestant experiment, which gave rise to the "open and affirming"

---

4 See *Empowered Evangelicals: Bringing Together the Best of the Evangelical and Charismatic Worlds*, by Rich Nathan and Ken Wilson. Garden City, Idaho: Ampelon Publishing, 2009.

position. One could say it emerged as a reaction to Liberal Protestantism.

Liberal Protestantism, in turn, was a response to modernity—the rise of science and the willingness to subject sacred text to historical and textual criticism. Liberal Protestantism engaged the modern world sympathetically. It seemed to embrace, even at times to revel in, doubting the core aspects of Christian dogma, like the resurrection, the heart of Christianity. [5] (I say "seemed to" because I am not an insider to Liberal Protestantism. I'm chastened by knowing how my own faith can be misjudged by those whose knowledge of it is unsympathetic and shallow.) And yet my narrative as an evangelical, supported by many who don't have a dog in the fight, views Liberal Protestantism as a failed experiment, one that is associated with the steep membership declines that hastened my own exit from a tepid Episcopal parish in the 1960s.

The Jesus movement that brought me back to faith marked a return to the essential core of Christianity stripped of the institutional trappings of Christendom (or so we thought) with a laser-like focus on the crucified, risen, ascending and returning Jesus. I was all in then and am all in now. I think this caution about the origins of the "open and affirming" position has led me to a more substantial critique of that position than *simply* guilt by association. I like its emphasis on inclusion—my instinct tells me Jesus would expect us to err and would prefer that we err on the side of inclusion—but I'm concerned about how this approach shapes our understanding of the gospel.

The alternative to the "open and affirming" position had its problems too, which took longer to appreciate in my case. Even in its soft form, the traditional "love the sinner, hate the sin" position insists on excluding gay people from *something*. As time goes on, the traditional position will

---

5 A contemporary writer who represents this perspective in my mind is Bishop John Shelby Spong.

soften further—that is, it will insist on excluding gay people from less and less—but it will always demand some form of exclusion. As I began to meet more gay people in my pastoral role, to sit down with them face-to-face and grapple with the consequences of actually hating their sin, it just didn't *feel* like a Jesus approach.

This discomfort led me to scrutinize the traditional position more closely. I came to distrust the capacity of most people to hate the sin while loving the sinner. Without question, "love the sinner, hate the sin" is a helpful aphorism to deal with egregious forms of evil. It enables us to love our enemies when their sin harms us. But it doesn't seem helpful in many other situations—for loving one's spouse, who is a sinner, for example.

"I love you, but I hate your overeating" doesn't help a marriage. It's not helpful because hatred is a powerful emotion (a posture, really) that is not easy to wield or maintain carefully. Hatred is more a bludgeon than a scalpel. Our ability to distinguish sin from sinner, especially in others, is so limited, so vulnerable to our own unexamined subjectivity.

I'll say more about this later, but as my contact with gay people increased, my pastoral instincts told me that the traditional approach didn't *fit* them or their circumstances well.

My Discomfort with My Own Discomfort

Right away, these thoughts generated anxiety in me. As I tentatively shared my concerns with pastor colleagues, I sensed the strain. I think we, meaning my denomination and every other organized form of American Evangelicalism, are an anxious system in which it's not easy to discuss this issue with the gentleness, calm, and candor that pastoral matters require. Once my concerns took definite shape and suggested a different trajectory in my thinking, the tension only increased. This controversy has strained my relationships with many of my colleagues, in some cases severely.

In so many religious settings, as soon as one subjects the traditional consensus to greater scrutiny, a dividing line manifests and people find themselves in two separate camps—somehow beyond the circle of friendship formed by the attractive power of Jesus among us as a friend. I don't expect my pastoral colleagues to agree with me—many, surely, will not, and have told me as much. In fact, one young pastor recently met up with me in the lobby at our national conference and said (in good humor), "I was a little nervous to be seen with you since you've become a pariah around here." I laughed … and winced.

But some matters are unavoidable and this is one of them, at least in Ann Arbor, where I live. The church I serve as a pastor is seeking to bear witness in a left-leaning, environment- and science-friendly, religiously averse community, home to a large secular research institution, the University of Michigan. My spiritual director, Don Postema, [6] who led the Christian Reformed Campus Chapel in Ann Arbor for more than thirty years, told me, "Being a pastor in a college town is like serving on the mission outpost of the future. Here, you face issues that will eventually catch up to everyone, but have arrived at your doorstep in advance."

This issue arrived at my doorstep several years ago. It has arrived at the doorstep of every other pastor in the country by now. Avoiding it has always had consequences for gay people. But now consequences are unavoidable for local congregations as well, since so many congregants know more openly gay people. Exclusionary practices have consequences—many of the young in these congregations find them abhorrent. Abandoning the exclusionary practices has consequences— many of the long-time members find this equally abhorrent. Several years ago, thanks to my living in a university town, "the gay issue" seemed to be chiding me in a "Ready or not,

---

6 Don is the author of *Space for God*, a treasure of contemplative prayer in the Reformed tradition. He served for a year as personal assistant to Henri Nouwen at Yale.

here I come" sort of way. I decided to engage it, and this is the account of that engagement.

Stumbling Into a Process of Discernment

I understand discernment in the context of a framework pressed out by Ignatius of Loyola, founder of the Society of Jesus. I went through the first year of an internship in Ignatian Spirituality at the Manresa Retreat House in Detroit, led by Father Bernie Owens, S.J., with a couple of others from our church. We now have our own Spiritual Direction program, where we train spiritual directors in this method for service in the local church and beyond. In the Ignatian model, discernment of God's will is reserved for choosing between two or more possible goods. [7] When faced with a choice between a good and an evil option, no discernment is needed. Choose the good and shun the evil.

For many years, long before I was familiar with Ignatian discernment, I didn't view the question of how the church should respond to people engaged in homosexual acts or relationships as a matter to be "discerned." As I first encountered the question of homosexuality, I saw it as a simple matter of choosing faithfulness to God over unfaithfulness to God.

Hard as it may seem to imagine now, I was married before I learned what gay men did for sex. When I found out, I was quite surprised. The early Jesus movement (in the late 1960s early 1970s) didn't pay attention to homosexuality one way or another, at least not in my neck of the Jesus movement in Detroit and in Ann Arbor ... at first.

In my first twenty years of pastoral ministry, I only knew people (men mostly) who were distressed by their same-sex orientation. As the issue became more prominent during the

---

7 In the Ignation method, a choice between good and evil does not require a process of discernment. Choose the good, shun the evil. See Gallagher, Timothy. *Discerning the Will of God.* New York, N.Y.: The Crossroad Publishing Co., 2009, pp. 16-17.

coincident rise of the Gay Rights movement and the Religious Right, I assumed (of course) that all homosexual acts and relationships were outside the bounds of morally acceptable behavior. For me, this was a received tradition. It came with a set of exclusionary practices, but I didn't examine the practices carefully for two reasons: 1) at first, I wasn't personally in charge of excluding anyone, and 2) when I was, exclusion *per se* didn't need to be exercised because gay people who wanted to remain gay stayed away.

I should emphasize: everyone I respected held this view; no one I respected questioned it. I had other pressing pastoral concerns. It didn't occur to me to explore the matter further.

My study of the relevant biblical texts on homosexuality amounted to simply reading them with an assist from a favorite commentary. During the 1990s, our church was located in Milan, Michigan, a small blue-collar community south of Ann Arbor. We did our best to help the few people that we knew who struggled with homosexuality. I last taught publically on the topic in 1997—rehearsing my understanding of the biblical teaching on homosexuality. This included a few items. First, I said that all homosexual acts are not to be treated as a special category of heinous sin (despite teaching to the contrary in the Christian tradition); second, that "gay bashing" is bad and we should have nothing to do with it; third, that homosexual orientation *per se* is not sinful (also contrary to some traditional teaching); and then finally, that all homosexual acts are prohibited by the clear teaching of Scripture. For years in our membership class, I took a few minutes to clarify the Christian teaching on homosexuality: those in active gay relationships should end them before joining the church, with pastoral assistance offered, but rarely requested.

After we planted the church in Ann Arbor in 2001, I noticed a change. With increasing frequency, church members quietly acknowledged having close family members who were gay. Were things changing so rapidly or was this just coming out into the open? I wasn't sure. Later, even closer to home, I began to hear from Christian parents concerned about adolescent children who thought they were gay. All this was new.

Eventually, I met more openly gay people who didn't seem to be conflicted about their sexuality. Some had entered monogamous partnerships in which they intended to practice exclusive fidelity. A few were raising children together. Their circumstances were very new to me. When I reviewed the traditional case against homosexuality with some of my own children it didn't resonate with them. I could make a compelling case against sexual immorality in the form of adultery, one that made sense to them. I could advocate sexual abstinence before covenantal commitment with conviction and get a fair hearing. But this other issue was different: my arguments boiled down to "because the Bible says so." It was much harder to marshal confirming reasons, the things a parent says when trying to help a child understand *why* the Bible might say something. Maybe my own untested convictions were affecting my powers of persuasion. Or perhaps I had my own latent doubts to face. [8]

My wife and I came to know and love people who are gay through our involvement in high school athletics and extracurricular activities. (Nancy was head coach of the high school equestrian team and our youngest daughter was active in two sports.) These individuals did not fit the picture of homosexuality presented in media coverage of Gay Pride parades, or what we read of in Scripture. Some were parents. One became the most positive influence in our daughter's

---

8 For example, I read *The Future of Marriage* by David Blankenthorn, who advances a case against gay marriage on the grounds that it undermines marriage and childrearing in society. I found myself unpersuaded. Later, the author did an op-ed piece in the *New York Times* in which he withdrew his objections to gay marriage. See: Oppenheimer, Mark. *In Shift, an Activist Enlists Same-Sex Couples in a Pro-Marriage Coalition.* New York Times, January 29, 2013.

life at the time. They especially did not fit the seminal
homosexuality text in the first chapter of Romans. I couldn't
but re-examine my previously settled convictions.

It's one thing to adopt a position on controversial questions
like divorce and remarriage, Christian participation in war,
entering a lawsuit against a fellow believer, or the use of in
vitro fertilization, but it's another to field test them in real life.
As a pastor I face these questions with those for whom they
are not abstractions. It makes you more careful in your moral
judgments.

Many moral questions, thankfully, are quite clear. That
clarity is reassuring and necessary in a sin-soaked world. Life
is complicated enough without seeking out more complexity.
But other moral questions *are* more challenging to sort out,
especially when they are personal and particular, not abstract.
The more pastoral experience I had, the more I saw moral
dilemmas where others saw none.

An Early Experience with a Transgender Person

I had a jarring introduction to this complexity when I met
with a man who disclosed to me that he was a newly baptized
believer from another church who had undergone transgender
surgery to become a man. His home church had known of
this transition, baptized him, then later insisted that he revert
to the gender of his birth. This would have involved extensive,
expensive and multiple surgeries with a dubious surgical
outcome. "What should I do?" he asked.

Of course, I wanted to hear more of his story. I was buying
time as much as anything. Trained as a registered nurse, I
was familiar with the reality of ambiguously gendered people,
including those whose gender ambiguity was reflected in their
DNA, as well as those who identified profoundly with one
gender while having the genitalia of another. [9] I hadn't sorted
out what light the Bible might shine on his situation, but as he

---

9 See: Callahan, Gerald N. *Between XX and XY: Intersexuality and
the Myth of Two Sexes.* Chicago, Ill: Chicago Review Press, 2009,

filled in the details of his story, I scanned my Bible knowledge for help. I admitted to him that I hadn't dealt with this before and that my initial responses would be just that. We pastors have to do our theology on the fly sometimes.

Taking a deep breath, I dove in. My job as a pastor was not to determine his gender. It was his job as a child of God to tell me what his gender was. I told him that in the Bible there is a progression regarding the treatment of eunuchs, who would be the closest equivalent of transgender people today. This progression went from excluding them from temple worship (Deuteronomy 23:1), to the anticipation of their acceptance in the Hebrew prophets (Isaiah 56:4), to the recognition of a place in the kingdom of God for eunuchs in the ministry of Jesus (Matthew 19:12) and the inclusive practice of the early church in the book of Acts (Acts 8:27-39).

Hearing this man's story gave a face to the disconcerting issue of gender change. I saw the anguish that led him to such an extreme step. I saw that the moral questions raised by his experience were not in the "crystal clear" category.

The Remarriage Dilemma, Another Turning Point

I already had experience with the complex moral questions that required my discernment. The divorce and remarriage question taught me this. It comes up a lot when I speak to other pastors about the care of people who are gay and lesbian. I'll speak of it now and return to it later because my struggle with this question has powerfully shaped my thinking as a pastor about homosexuality.

In the early 1980s, I studied divorce and remarriage extensively with my fellow pastor at the time, Mark Kinzer, now a leader in the Messianic Jewish movement and a respected scholar of Second Temple Judaism. Mark was a dear friend from high school and we came to faith in Jesus together as freshmen at the University of Michigan. Now as co-pastors,

---

for an excellent introduction to the medical conditions involved in transgenderism.

we were in our early thirties, but without much experience in matters of marriage, divorce, and remarriage. Mark was part of a brotherhood of men committed to celibacy. I was married to my high-school sweetheart. We searched the Scriptures, the teaching of the early church fathers, and the development of teaching through church history on this question. And we concluded that the early church had this question essentially right—that there were no clear-cut biblical exceptions to the no marriage after divorce rule, [10] other than the death of one's spouse. We acknowledged the Reformers' later inclusion of

---

10 Romans 7:2-3 For the woman who has a husband is bound by the law to her husband so long as he lives; but if the husband is dead, she is loosed from the law of her husband. So then if, while her husband lives, she is married to another man, she shall be called an adulteress: but if her husband is dead, she is free from that law; so that she is no adulteress, though she is married to another man.

Matthew 19:6 "Wherefore they are no more two, but one flesh. What therefore God has joined together, let not man put asunder."

Mark 10:2-12 And the Pharisees came to him, and asked him, Is it lawful for a man to put away his wife? Tempting him. And he answered and said unto them, What did Moses command you? And they said, Moses suffered to write a bill of divorcement, and to put her away. And Jesus answered and said unto them, For the hardness of your heart he wrote you this precept. But from the beginning of the creation God made them male and female. For this cause shall a man leave his father and mother, and cleave to his wife; And they two shall be one flesh: so then they are no more two, but one flesh. What therefore God hath joined together, let not man put asunder. And in the house his disciples asked him again of the same matter. And he sad to them, Whosoever shall put away his wife, and marry another, commits adultery against her. And if a woman shall put away her husband, and be married to another, she commits adultery.

Luke 16:18 Whosoever puts away his wife, and marries another, commits adultery: and whosoever marries her that is put away from her husband commits adultery.

the very narrow exceptions in the case of marital infidelity
and desertion, but viewed these as something other than
indisputably established with respect to remarriage. To play
it safe—and we wanted to—we decided to follow the clear
no-remarriage-after-divorce rule.

Mark went on to found a Messianic Jewish congregation,
while I assumed primary leadership for the church that
eventually became the Vineyard Church of Ann Arbor. I
encountered more and more divorced and remarried people
for whom the teaching didn't seem to fit. I felt the pangs
of conflicted conscience as I presented a strict view of the
grounds for remarriage after divorce in situations where my
emerging pastoral instinct said, "Something is not adding up
here."

Relentlessly, though, people in dissolving marriages came
to my office in need of help. People were always on the brink
of a decision. What would I advise? In the most difficult cases,
I wanted to offer to get back to them much later, perhaps after
the next millennium. Instead, I learned to go with my best
discernment in a given situation.

A newcomer meeting I had some years ago highlighted the
shift I'd undergone through my discernment process on the
issue of remarriage after divorce. A couple that had left our
church many years earlier returned and filled out a newcomer
card. I arranged to meet them one morning. In prayer before
the day's work began, the Spirit informed me (in no uncertain
terms) that I was to open the meeting with an apology.

The last time we had met (many years before) the woman,
a divorced single mom, came with her fiancé to ask whether I
would perform the wedding ceremony. Knowing their history,
I explained, as graciously as I could, that I would not be able
to participate because I was not certain that remarriage was
a faithful option in their case. They were very gracious in

---

1 Corinthians 7:39 The wife is bound by the law as long as her husband
lives; but if her husband be dead, she is at liberty to be married to
whom she will; only in the Lord.

response. And of course, they found a new church, in which they were married.

So this second meeting, many years later, began with my apology: "The last time we met you asked me to perform your wedding and I declined. I can see now that God has indeed blessed your marriage and that it was undertaken in faithfulness to God, despite my misgivings. I'm not sorry so much for my convictions at the time as I am for my posture at the time, which was to play it safe. These are difficult questions and I was your pastor, but I was unwilling to discern with you. And you deserved better than that. I am so sorry."

Their eyes filled with tears, but also with a look of wonder. "Ken, do you have any idea what day this is?"

I said, "Tuesday."

To which they replied, "No! Not what day of the week, what day in our *lives*? This is our twenty-fifth wedding anniversary today. Did you know that?" (I didn't.) "You have given us a wonderful gift."

Some moral questions don't require much discernment. Whether a husband cheating on his wife is being faithful to God does not require a lengthy process of moral discernment. He is committing adultery, a first-order sin forbidden in the Ten Commandments and throughout Scripture. His actions self-evidently harm his relationship with God, his wife and children, his community. But other moral questions do require a discernment process, including ones in which a great deal is at stake. Whether a divorced person becomes an adulterer through remarriage (this *is* the concern raised in Scripture) requires a process of moral discernment.

Pastors accumulate a great deal of experience with difficult moral questions. People come to us for counsel and they tend to bring the tough situations, not the easy ones. While the Bible does speak clearly on many matters—you'd have to be deaf not to hear the condemnations of murder, stealing, adultery, greed, etc.—there are, in fact, many questions at the margins of each of these, for which there are not clear answers.

If you are not a pastor it's easier to maintain the comforting illusion that these hard cases are rare. But they are not.

At the risk of belaboring the point, let me emphasize this. Murder, clearly wrong. No debate about that. But is killing in war murder? Huge debate. And the question is murder, not some secondary moral concern. Adultery, the Bible speaks with great clarity on this: "Thou shalt not commit adultery." A command, not a suggestion. But is remarriage after divorce adultery? If so, under what circumstances? This is not something you have to think about unless you are divorced, and then you only have to consider your own situation. Perhaps you've had a divorced friend ask, "I wonder if I'm allowed to remarry, given what the Bible says?" But honestly, if you are not a pastor, how often have you *actually* been asked that question? And if you have, how much effort did you put into providing a credible answer that deals with all complexities involved?

Welcome to my world. I've been a pastor for close to forty years, caring for people who are conscientious about their faith and want to do what's right. And they have come to me, often in a state of moral distress, to ask their tough questions. They don't have other people to go to. Their friends empathize with them but tell them they should talk to a pastor. Their therapists help them sort out their feelings about the issue, but questions of morality? They defer to a clergy person on that. I'm the clergy person expected to answer the question. And now, after decades of pastoral experience, I am convinced, and when I say convinced I mean I think this is true and I feel in my bones that it is true: while the Bible speaks clearly on many moral issues, there are also plenty of questions for which there are not clear answers. These questions are often aspects of the big moral concerns, too: stealing, murder, adultery, and the like. People who know God and the Bible better than me spend enormous energy seeking answers to these difficult questions and come up with conflicting opinions.

I began to see the question of homosexuality in a new light. I couldn't shake the thought that if we applied the same pastoral consideration to gay people that we give to the divorced and remarried, we'd come up with something much different than the categorical exclusions from church and ministry that we have practiced.

Yes, I needed to dig into this further. Simple fairness demanded it.

Facing the Effects of Exclusion

Placing the traditional exclusionary approach under greater scrutiny only heightened my concerns. These policies in their various iterations—exclusion from membership, disqualification from leadership—even when softened with contemporary compassionate language, seemed harmful.

Before serving as a pastor, I worked as a registered nurse in community mental health, so research in this field interests me. One study surveyed several congregations. It found gay teenagers in every congregation. If the congregation took the "love the sinner, hate the sin" approach, the kids kept their sexuality a secret from pastors and youth workers. [11] Kids in these settings were at greater risk for self-harm, including suicide. [12] These findings are especially troubling, since

11 Clapp, Steve., Leverton Helbert, Kristen., and Zizak Angela. *Faith Matters: Teenagers, Religion & Sexuality* (LifeQuest Growing in Faith Series). Bellevue, Wash.: LifeQuest, 2003 pp. 93-110.

12 Gay Christian youth with a high religious guidance had the greatest risk of non-suicidal self injury, increased likelihood of suicidal thoughts or attempts compared to heterosexual counterparts; seculars had moderate risk; and Christians with low religious guidance had the least risk. Higher levels of religiosity have also been associated with a few negative psychosocial outcomes such as increased levels of guilt, higher levels of authoritarianism and higher levels of fear and alienation, higher levels of scrupulosity and increased levels of depression among certain groups. Joseph Longo, N. Eugene Walls and Hope Wisneski. Religion and religiosity: protective or harmful factors

normally church affiliation is associated with *improved* mental health. The study squared with a nagging intuition I had and with my own experience raising five children through the turbulent years of adolescence.

After decades without a parent asking me about an adolescent or adult child coming out as gay, a string of parents set up appointments with me to discuss this. Strangely, each time, I knew in advance, by the Spirit, what their concern was, despite their not revealing it beforehand. By this time, I'd done some homework, so I shared some of the insights I had gained and it seemed to provide enormous relief. I told of the lack of evidence for the common theory that homosexuality is caused by a distant father and an over-involved mother, and the growing body of evidence that nature plays a powerful but complex role in same-sex orientation. [13]

Whereas before I might have offered assurance that this was like any other sinful temptation, I told these parents that I wasn't convinced it was that simple in this case. The parents relaxed as I shared my reflections. When it involved their own child, they shared the same instinct about the "love the sinner, hate the sin" approach that I had.

I told them that the more I knew of the experience of gay people, the less likely it seemed to me that kids would come out to parents about this. Even in a liberal town like Ann Arbor, kids are not eager to be known as gay. They didn't tend to acknowledge it casually. Despite the growing acceptance of homosexuality in our society, the kids were facing powerful

---

for sexual minority youth? *Mental Health, Religion & Culture*, 2013 Vol. 16, No. 3, 273-290.

13 After literally two years searching for a good scientific book on the topic, during which time I asked for recommendations from high-level scientists, including the then-director of the U.S. Center for Disease Control (long story) and having them draw a blank, I discovered this excellent summary of scientific research on the question: Wilson, Glenn and Rahman, Qazi. *Born Gay: The Psychobiology of Sex Orientation*. London, UK: Peter Owen Ltd, 2008.

social pressure *not* to be gay. I encouraged parents to adopt a wait-and-see posture. Don't be quick to define a child's orientation. Sexual orientation, especially in adolescence, isn't always firmly fixed (though it can be). [14] But the longer a teenager's same-sex attraction continues, the greater the likelihood that it will persist for a lifetime.

Some parents shared their previously unspoken observations: "Yes, he told us that he's been holding on to this secret for years. That he'd tried hard to feel otherwise." Or, "You know, it was shock to hear, but we weren't really surprised. We wondered if she leaned that way even when she was very young."

Often these parents seemed caught between conflicting perspectives. On the one hand, they said, "I know it's no worse than other sins." But their facial expressions said, "Is something horribly wrong with my child?" Seeing the anguish of some parents sensitized me to the harmful aspects of the Christian tradition that are no longer trumpeted. But their effects linger.

This led me to describe some of the factors fueling the intense aversion to homosexuality in the tradition. Until recently, "sodomy" was the polite term for anal intercourse. But the use of that word is based on a misunderstanding of the story of Sodom and Gomorrah in Genesis 19 (and a similar story in Judges 19). [15] In these accounts, the crime was

---

14 See *Faith Matters*, Clapp et al, p. 95 "Some sexuality education professionals report that as many as 25 percent of twelve-year-olds are unsure of their sexual orientation but that only 5 percent of eighteen-year-olds have that same uncertainty."

15 "The notorious story of Sodom and Gomorrah—often cited in connection with homosexuality—is actually irrelevant to the topic … there is nothing in the passage that is pertinent to a judgment about the morality of consensual homosexual intercourse … In fact, the clearest statement about the sin of Sodom is to be found in an oracle of the prophet Ezekiel: 'This was the guilt of your sister Sodom: she and her daughters had pride, excess of food, and prosperous ease, but did

attempted gang rape, a crime of violence attempted by "the whole town", not a few men with same-sex orientation. In Judges, the eventual victims were women, not men.

Yet "sodomy," I explained to the parents of gay children, appeared in the influential Authorized Version, translated from the Hebrew, *kadesh*, in Deuteronomy 23:17 and elsewhere. This Hebrew word has nothing to do with the biblical town of Sodom. Later translations, including the bestselling New International Version, use the term "shrine prostitute" instead. Yet even the New Revised Standard Version still uses "sodomite" to translate the Greek word *arsenokoitai* in 1 Corinthians 6:9, despite the fact that this Greek word has nothing to do with the town of Sodom. "Sodomy," enshrined in the "anti-sodomy" statutes in the United States, links the story about the abhorrent evil of the townsmen of Sodom with all homosexuality.

I urged these parents to reflect on the disgust they were feeling at the thought that their kids may eventually want to have gay sex. When a person doesn't feel the same sexual attractions that another person feels, those other feelings seem "unnatural." School-age children feel disgust when they learn what their parents did to get pregnant. All sex, when scrutinized, can be perceived as gross, especially to the non-participants. But the disgust response to homosexuality is heightened by the belief that all gay sex is as perverse as what those men in Sodom wanted to do to the visiting angels. This is deeply rooted in the Christian tradition going back to Thomas Aquinas, whose work had a huge impact on Western Christianity. Aquinas taught that homosexuality is worse than incest, a view that most conservative scholars deny today. [16] Nevertheless, while most scholars do not support these

---

not aid the poor and needy." (Hays, Richard. B. *The Moral Vision of The New Testament, A Contemporary Introduction to New Testament Ethics.* New York, N.Y.: HarperCollins, 1996, p. 381.)

16 St. Thomas Aquinas. *Summa Theologica*. Question 145. Among conservative scholars, I could only find Robert Gagnon making the

perspectives any longer, once such things are embedded in the Christian cultural matrix, they are not easy to dislodge.

The effect of this history, a history that has fueled the current controversy surrounding this issue, is to stigmatize people who are in same-sex relationships or want to be. This stigmatization is harmful to them and to the people who love them, like their parents.

Having this conversation about disgust seemed to dispel a dark cloud over these parents, a cloud that my gut told me was a demonic, not a godly, influence.

In the case of minor children still under the care of parents, the conversation turned to the question of boundaries. My counsel for these parents went something like this: "Gay or straight, high school is too soon for sexual intimacy. Sex isn't recreation. It forges deep bonds, not easily broken. The body is a temple. Your child has a lot to learn about herself and others before bonding in that deep way with another human being. Common sense for teenagers still applies: remind your child that sex isn't just about being horny, even at this age of raging hormones. Sex is for pair bonding. It's about finding someone to forge a deep bond of loyalty with—a mate who offers security through thick and thin. So be the parents and set healthy boundaries."

Talking with these parents helped me to see this issue through a different lens. How would I respond if one of my children or grandchildren came out as gay? What kind of church would I want for them?

Many of us haven't had to consider this question because we don't have a close family member who is openly gay. As a pastor, I couldn't avoid it. So I invite you to picture yourself as a parent to a teenage child who takes a big risk and shares with you that he or she has only known strong same-sex attraction, that it baffles them, that they have tried different

---

case that homosexual acts are worse than incest. I found his grounds unpersuasive. Gagnon, Robert A. J. *The Bible and Homosexual Practice.* Nashville, Tenn.; Abingdon Press, 2001.

strategies to experience what their friends do, to no avail. They are frightened, perhaps a little ashamed, because teenagers more than anything want to fit in with their peers. But most of all they are vulnerable. What would that be like?

I saw how some parents tried to implement the "love the sinner, hate the sin" approach with their own children in these circumstances. I saw how their kids (some of whom I knew to have a tender heart toward God) assumed that following Jesus and pleasing their parents was no longer possible. It felt as though parent and child regarded themselves as participants in a Greek tragedy—that despite their kinship bond, they could never be close again.

In my pastoral role with the parents of gay children, "love the sinner, hate the sin" lost its luster as a ready answer to the moral dimensions of the gay issue. All this was exploratory and I acknowledged as much to parents coming to me with their concerns. But they needed something, the best I could offer. Hearing my own words, feeling the conviction behind them, I realized that my views were shifting, had shifted. The "love the sinner, hate the sin" approach wasn't good enough. In practice, it was too harmful.

My re-think was informed by knowing some (not all) Christians with strong same-sex attraction, who married in an effort to overcome these unwanted attractions. Their powerful same-sex attraction didn't abate and impeded their ability to bond with their mate. Sometimes the marriages dissolved years later as a result. Evidence began to surface that the healing approach to same-sex orientation seemed to be overstated. (Recently, in fact, leaders in the ex-gay movement have split over the appropriate response to the growing evidence that, for many people who gave it their all, same-sex attraction didn't yield much to reparative approaches.) [17] Yet, while all this was unfolding, I knew some people for whom

---

17 http://exodusinternational.org/2013/06/
exodus-international-to-shut-down/

such ministries were helpful. Whatever this was, it wasn't simple.

Experience Changes One's Perspective

My heightened awareness of the harm caused by the traditional approach corresponded to a changing perspective on "the gay community" as a whole. In the evangelical subculture, I had absorbed the view that gays and lesbians were a privileged minority, working their will on the rest of us. But I began to see that as a stereotype. The more I looked into it, the more I saw gays and lesbians differently, as people with a burden to bear, even in a tolerant town like Ann Arbor.

For example, I met some students in the gay-straight alliance at a local Ann Arbor high school. The faculty sponsor of the alliance was a member of our church. The students had asked several other faculty members for help getting the group started and none wanted to be involved. I learned that gay students were subject to a great deal of ridicule in high school, even in liberal Ann Arbor. In fact, the students I met referred to themselves as "homosexual," since "gay" was used as a hurtful slur.

My daughter Grace was in a high school science class in which a student asked a devout Catholic teacher what he thought of homosexuality. The teacher said he thought it was morally disordered. A young student started to cry. My daughter knew that he identified as gay. Grace, always an advocate for the underdog, stood up and said, "Well, both my parents are pastors, and I don't know what they think about this, but I know that Jesus accepted all people!" The young student told her through wet eyes, "Grace, you're my hero!" I felt proud of Grace, too, and realized how much my perspective was changing.

I was powerfully affected by a weekend visit that Grace, Nancy and I took to the home of Sam and Phyllis Tickle, near Memphis, Tennesee. A renowned physician and lung specialist, Sam had been a first responder to the AIDS epidemic when

it hit Memphis. He cared for the most down-and-out gay
men and transgender people and had become their fierce and
compassionate advocate. He did so during the hysteria and
rank prejudice that attended the outbreak of the AIDS crisis in
the 1980s.

Sam and Phyllis took us to a worship service of mostly
gay, lesbian, hermaphrodite and transgender people who had
found refuge in their local church. These men and women
didn't fulfill my ill-informed media stereotype of a group of
upwardly mobile gay hipsters. They were society's outcasts.
The church building had been sprayed with bullets in drive-by
shootings. I went into the service with my spiritual antennae
up—and I discerned a powerful presence of Jesus that
surprised and deeply moved me. The difference between my
guarded fear and his presence was striking and humbling.

As I opened myself to new experience, my views shifted. I
could see that the exclusionary approach that kept these men
and women away from church, or kept them in hiding in the
church, was more harmful than helpful to them. I just didn't
see a way to implement the approach without imposing the
harm.

As I shared my growing concerns with other pastors,
their responses didn't fit what I was sensing. Some said, yes,
exclusion is hard, but gay people need to face the hard truth of
Scripture's prohibition. Jesus calls us to deny self, pick up our
cross and follow. Sometimes if it hurts, we're still supposed to
do it, out of faithfulness to Christ.

True, I thought, but does this truth pertain in the case of
these people? In any event, I knew this did not excuse me of
the responsibility to take the harm seriously. The people I was
getting to know just didn't seem like the hardened sinners for
whom the strong condemnations of Scripture were intended.

I became sensitized to the warning in Scripture against
imposing religious harm. Saul of Tarsus harmed others in
his zeal for truth. Perhaps for this reason, he stressed, "Love
does no harm to the neighbor" (Romans 13:10). With Jesus

and the other apostles, he *emphasized* love as the fulfillment of the Law and the prophets. Why this emphasis in the early Jesus movement, if not for the tendency to violate love in the pursuit of religious devotion? I couldn't simply ignore the harm associated with the traditional reading and application of Scripture. I couldn't outsource this. I had to do my own praying, studying, conversing, reflecting. I had to do my homework.

Along the way, I felt encouraged by the Spirit to continue, despite substantial fear. Why had I been given an uncannily accurate premonition when those first five or six parents made appointments with me to disclose that their child was coming out as gay? Was my research and deeper look into this issue *preparing* me to be a source of comfort from the Spirit to these parents? Were they coming to me now because I wasn't ready for them earlier?

The awareness of harm has only increased since I began this process. Our church includes many grad students and others who are familiar with survey research. They pass things on to me and help create an environment in which such research is respected. Just recently, I received—from a member of our church who works in academia, was raised evangelical and has a gay brother—a study by researchers at Yale. This study demonstrates that gays and lesbians in states that went through heightened controversy over efforts to ban gay marriage suffered a significant spike in psychiatric symptoms (depression, panic attacks, generalized anxiety and mood disorders, etc.) compared with gays and lesbians in other states during the same period and heterosexuals in their own states. [18]

---

18 Mark L. Hatzenbuehler, Katie A. McLaughlin, Katherine M. Keyes, and Deborah S. Hasin. *The Impact of Institutional Discrimination on Psychiatric Disorders in Lesbian, Gay, and Bisexual Populations: A Prospective Study*. American Journal of Public Health: March 2010, Vol. 100, No. 3, pp. 452-459.

As I raised my growing concerns with some pastor colleagues, I learned that some had been thinking along similar lines. Often, though, they *confided* their concerns to me.

Of course, many were alarmed when I revealed my shifting perspectives. We seemed to be operating from two different frames of pastoral reference. They spoke only of the brokenness of "the homosexual lifestyle." Of course, I knew of promiscuity and the manipulative or exploitative use of sexuality among gay people, but these same practices characterized much of heterosexuality as well. For whatever reason, I seemed to be encountering more gay people whose lives didn't fit that familiar pejorative, "the homosexual lifestyle."

Increasingly, the gay people I interacted with, like many straight people I know, had healthier instincts. They wanted to express their sexuality in a loving, faithful relationship that put the interests of others above raw self-interest. I saw people who knew that sex wasn't just a lustful itch to be scratched; like others, they knew that sex is part of the process of forging a pair-bond, the kind of intimacy that can see a person through thick and thin for a lifetime. When they didn't live up to a higher view of sexuality, just as so many heterosexual people don't, they wanted to.

Discernment in the Fires of Controversy

My year studying Ignatian spirituality came just in time to help me understand the discernment process I was already engaged in. Ignatius describes three modes of spiritual discernment. In Mode 1, one has a startlingly clear and undeniable revelation that settles the matter. This did not happen in my case. Mode 2 involves paying attention to the work of the good spirit and the bad spirit (spiritual consolations and desolations) as various options are considered. Depending on the issue, this can take months or years. This has been a major component of my discernment process. In Mode 3, one considers the various pros and cons of the available options. It can be done in conjunction with Mode 2 (as in my case) or when Mode 2 doesn't lead to a decision. My reading, getting to know gay people, and in-depth study of the Scripture were all part of Mode 3 discernment. Depending on the issue, one moves progressively through or between the modes in as unhurried a fashion as possible. [19] My process has taken years, not months.

It's been so arduous because it was so hard to even get my bearings, given how much pressure surrounds an evangelical pastor dealing with this.

It has included innumerable conversations with my wife, fellow pastors, other trusted colleagues and friends. Since this issue has become the focal point of a raging culture war, I had to tread carefully to see if there was openness to discussion. I serve on a pastoral team of people I trust deeply, and this trust was needed for these conversations —and they have been extensive. We took a full year to read and discuss some books together—this, after many informal conversations over a few years. I spoke openly with my church board as my concerns and engagement with this issue developed. I kept my two men's groups apprised, and they weighed in with their own thoughts. I have a close friend and walking partner who became a trusted sounding board, pushing back with questions and concerns of his own.

As I had opportunity, I spoke with other pastors within and beyond my denomination. I spoke with most of the people with whom I served on the Vineyard national board and with trusted pastor colleagues that I've known for years. Many were mildly alarmed by these conversations, knowing the intensity of the controversy surrounding this issue, and just what is at stake when a pastor develops concerns such as I had. Nearly every pastor said various versions of, "Ken, you do realize how contentious this issue is, how churches blow up and divide over things like this." As if I didn't know.

---

19 Gallagher, *Discerning the Will of God.* pp. 69-120.

Later in the process, our pastoral team has had one-on-one conversations with our larger circle of local church leaders (about 70) and others in the congregation. Early on, I decided not to process this in a congregational or "town hall meeting" format. The issues are so intensely personal and tender, and those who are gay have experienced such profound anguish from the atmosphere of controversy that surrounds this issue, that I didn't feel it was appropriate to do so. Our church hasn't handled any number of sensitive moral questions in this way. I felt that to do so with this one would only add to the stigmatization already inflicted on gay people by the church.

Sorting through my thinking and praying over this became a major part of my spiritual direction meetings. Furthermore, I met with a Christian counselor to talk over some struggles I was having with anxiety—and this issue kept surfacing.

I've read scores of books, searching out the many related questions that a pastor must consider. One time, Nancy and I were looking for a book on scientific research on homosexuality and transgender in Borders Bookstore. We asked a clerk for help and she directed us to the "erotica" section. So there we were, two evangelical pastors browsing the erotica section. Periods of wrestling alternated with periods of putting the question on the shelf. Did I mention this is the most vexing question I have ever dealt with?

The reasons for my anguish are obvious: the traditional consensus of the church is not something to trifle with. The claim to harm can be made on both sides of the question. I know men who have experienced strong same-sex attraction but are committed either to lifelong celibacy or to making a heterosexual marriage work. These are commitments I wish to honor, not undermine. I don't believe that there is a "one size fits all" approach to this or to many other issues like this. Jesus knows the sheep of his pasture and leads each one of us in ways that are perfectly suited to our "never been before" identity as unique human beings. The dynamics of controversy run roughshod over that.

And … this *is* the mother of all church-splitting controversies, fueled by the flames of intense media and political focus in a decades-long culture war that has deeply affected American Christianity. One's position on this issue now seems to be regarded as a litmus test for orthodoxy. Dealing with this question has strained my relationship with my denomination, a community of churches that I love dearly. The confession "Jesus is Lord" is not enough, it seems, to hold people together who disagree on this question. Confessing the historic faith of the great ecumenical creeds is not enough. To be fully accepted, one must adopt the correct position on this vexing moral question. Not long ago, a close pastor friend (not from my own denomination) rebuked me for "getting soft on the gay issue" when we met for breakfast. Pastors within my denomination told me that if our church embraced an inclusive approach to gay people, many other churches would leave our denomination in protest.

The sheer pressure of threatened separation over this one issue—from members of one's own church or from colleagues in one's larger church network—is enormous. The question I had to ask in the context of spiritual discernment was this: Is the pressure from God? Which spirit is behind the pressure? Is the pressure something to yield to or something to ignore?

I don't think I would have been able to identify, let alone resist this pressure, were it not for the intense consolation that I experienced in prayer over a year-and-a-half. This took place at the beginning of my wrestling over this question. During this time, it seemed as though every experience of morning prayer was more rich and deeply intimate than any day's prayer in my preceding decades of daily prayer. (It was out of this remarkable period that I developed the material in *Mystically Wired: Exploring New Realms in Prayer*.) [20]

Occasionally, I've been challenged by someone saying, "Is all this grief worth it? Other thorny questions affect a lot more

---

20 Wilson, Ken. *Mystically Wired: Exploring New Realms in Prayer.* Nashville, Tenn.: Thomas Nelson, 2009.

people than this one does." It's a compelling consideration. Leading a church takes a lot of effort and focus. I had to ask myself, "Am I simply getting distracted by this?" I even took a break from thinking or talking about the issue for an Advent season (at the recommendation of my spiritual director). When Advent was over, the concern hadn't gone away.

I found my way forward by returning time and again to my duty as a pastor. As a pastor, I have a responsibility to Jesus to care for his sheep to the best of my ability. I simply couldn't shake the growing conviction that enforcing the traditional exclusion of gay people seemed inconsistent with that duty.

Heeding the Mission Alarm

Two concerns have motivated me: the harm to gay people associated with the traditional exclusionary approach *and* the harm that this approach does to the Christian mission in Ann Arbor. The fact is, I have been *driven* by a sense of mission in this discernment process. I mentioned this earlier but want to elaborate on it further. We decided to plant a church in Ann Arbor after I received what I believe to be Jesus' heart for lost sheep, especially those in communities like Ann Arbor. This extended move of the Spirit in my heart, over a period of several months with attendant tears, at times intercessory wailing and the like, was undeniable and caught my attention.

Our church had become less effective in reaching younger generations as the 1990s wore on. And we were more effective than any church in town, which might have masked my concern, but for the Spirit's awakening work. But the fact is, we were slowly aging. We were noticing what has now been demonstrated by demographic studies—that the church, including its evangelical wing, is losing, not attracting, young people at alarming rates; the rate of decline is less than the loss of young baby boomers in the 1960s, but it has been going on longer. And the historical pattern is sobering: once a generational cohort is lost like this, even strong renewal movements don't restore the losses. [21]

We experienced this in a small working class town then. Now we were back in Ann Arbor, where these dynamics are accelerated by higher rates of education, more advanced secularity, and a more robust progressive social conscience. I was familiar with the analysis of *Why Conservative Churches are Growing*, by Dean Kelley, written in 1972. [22] I didn't see it working in Ann Arbor in 2001 (and less so today).

My openness to pursuing matters like environmental stewardship, rethinking the faith-based suspicion of evolution, pursuing ethnic, racial and cultural diversity, resisting the culture-war framing of modern American Christianity, advocating for the inclusion of women at all levels of leadership, and promoting contemplative forms of prayer is rooted, I believe, in this experienced work of the Spirit. In a place like Ann Arbor, an evangelical faces a choice between making the gospel known and hewing to the evangelical cultural tradition on such matters, including the gay issue.

In April 2013, CBS News reported that Washtenaw County, where Ann Arbor is located, had the greatest networking support in the country for marriage equality, measured by things like people using the marriage equality logo for their profile picture on Facebook. [23]

People here view any exclusionary policies toward gay people as unjust, a moral wrong. They want nothing to do with organizations that do such things. They see the church making accommodations for the divorced and remarried, and for many other things condemned in

---

21 Putnam, Robert. D and Campbell, David. E. *American Grace: How Religion Divides Us.* New York, N.Y.: Simon & Schuster, 2010.

22 Kelley, Dean M. *Why Conservative Churches are Growing: A Study in Sociology of Religion.* New York, N.Y.: Harper & Row, Publishers, 1972.

23 Ngak, Chenda. *Facebook releases map of marriage equality support. CBS News, March 29, 2013.*

Scripture, while enforcing exclusionary policies against gay people. Increasingly, these gay people are their dear friends, co-workers and family members. And they ask, "Is the church willing to exclude one group but not the other because LGBT people are a small minority group that the church can do without?" Causing an *unnecessary* disincentive to follow Christ is a serious offense, at least as serious as failing to uphold a moral good. It would be easy to ignore or dismiss this concern if I didn't think it had substantial merit.

My wife, who died unexpectedly in 2012, had a gift of "discernment of spirits" that I came to trust deeply. She had the uncanny ability to know the right thing to do in muddled situations. As I mentioned earlier, Nancy had many lesbian friends. Her heart told her that exclusion wasn't the answer, full embrace was. She had not worked out all the loose ends. Apparently, she thought that was my task.

I Had to Face It: My Predisposition Had Shifted

Try as we might, it is difficult to approach moral questions without a pre-existing lean. Often, we're not aware of our predispositions in moral matters. It is natural to assume good motives for our own (unrecognized) moral predispositions while suspecting the motive of those with differing ones. We readily assign ourselves the benefit of the doubt and withhold it from others. But our moral sense is not planted from above, distinct from our human flesh. [24] Grasping for the knowledge of good and evil effected our ancestors' original separation from God. Our moral sense suffers a deep alienation, a

---

24 Jewett, commenting on Romans 2:16: "There is not hint in this passage that Paul thought of conscience as the direct voice of God. Rather the conscience is viewed as the autonomous capacity within humans that marks their consistency with whatever moral standard they have internalized." Jewett, Paul. *Christian Tolerance, Paul's Message to the Modern Church*. Philadelphia, Pa.: The Westminster Press, 1982 p. 57)

pervasive distortion, and this is carried over into our religious lives. [25]

We can correct for this distortion, in part, by recognizing what our predisposition is and trying to honestly account for where it comes from. Many powerful factors resisted my shift. But when I examined them in spiritual direction, I discerned that fear played a prominent role. Would I lose the respect of trusted colleagues? Would I be asking for trouble in my local church when I should be planning for retirement, not a career change? Was I being misled by misplaced compassion? The views of trusted authorities, friends, and colleagues are internalized views that affect us deeply. Seeing my progression on this issue through their eyes was sometimes unnerving. Each of these fears needed sorting.

Where was my willingness to question the traditional consensus coming from? Did I have a perverse interest in rocking the boat for its own sake? Was I harboring resentments against authority? Did I have a desire to play the hero? Did I have some attraction to being an outlier? I discussed these matters with my spiritual director.

But the answers to these questions notwithstanding, I had shifted. I wanted to see if I could find a biblically thoughtful, faithful approach that would allow us to make space for gay men and women seeking Christ without renouncing commitments they had made to their partners in monogamous relationships. This became my lean.

Where has this taken me?

---

25 Bonhoeffer, Dietrich. *Ethics.* New York, N.Y.: The MacMillan Co., 1965 pp 17-20.

CHAPTER 3

A Closer Look at the Prohibitive Texts

Finding My Way to a Third Way

WE DO OUR best Bible reading full of questions, turning to Scripture with a sense of a need, a longing to discover something of the mind and heart of God. With a fresh set of questions and concerns, I undertook a closer study than I had ever conducted of the biblical texts pertaining directly to homosexuality.

I am a follower of Jesus. His book is my book. My assumption regarding Scripture (going in and coming out of this study) is that "All scripture is given by inspiration of God, and is profitable for doctrine, for reproof, for correction, for instruction in righteousness" (2 Timothy 3:16). I have invested too much of my life in seeking to be faithful to that witness to abandon it now.

But Jesus also had a way of reading Scripture that was surprising, unconventional, and paradoxical. This is part of what first fascinated me about Jesus in the gospels. His reading of Scripture got him into trouble. Getting into trouble is not a goal in our reading of Scripture (with whom and for what?) but we cannot rule it out as a possible consequence at times. Perhaps for this reason I've always been attracted to movements (the Jesus movement, the charismatic renewal movement, and the Vineyard) that began, for their time and context, with non-traditional readings of Scripture. This has left me open (one might say vulnerable) to considering such readings.

It was some time before I dove into a thorough and systematic study of the relevant texts. I knew they condemned same-sex acts without exception. But now it was time to study these texts carefully, in light of my growing experience as a pastor.

Why let my concerns percolate before going straight to a more in-depth study? I had read the texts on divorce and remarriage differently after walking with people through the complexities and anguish of divorce. Only experience pressed me to scrutinize the text and my assumptions about the text more carefully. As a result, I trust my reading of Scripture more—it feels more honest to me—when I give myself the space to let some cognitive dissonance arise (between what I think Scripture says and what I understand by experience). It made me a better pastor to my divorced congregants and I felt I owed the same to my gay and lesbian neighbors.

The Bible addresses same-sex activity a handful of times [26] (in Leviticus 18, [27] 20, [28] Romans 1, [29] 1 Corinthians 6, [30] 1 Timothy 1 [31]). A few other references do not provide any clear

---

26 In *A Moral Vision of the New Testament*, Richard Hays introduces his review of the prohibitive texts by saying, "The Bible hardly ever discusses homosexual behavior. There are perhaps half a dozen brief references to it in all of Scripture. In terms of emphasis, it is a minor concern. The paucity of texts addressing the issue is a significant fact for New Testament ethics." p. 381

27 Leviticus 18:22: Thou shall not lie with mankind, as with womankind: it is abomination.

28 Leviticus 20:13: If a man also lie with mankind, as he lies with a woman, both of them have committed an abomination: they shall surely be put to death; their blood shall be upon them.

29 Romans 1:24-27: Wherefore God also gave them up to uncleanness through the lusts of their own hearts, to dishonour their own bodies between themselves: Who changed the truth of God into a lie, and worshipped and served the creature more than the Creator, who is blessed for ever. Amen. For this cause God gave them up unto vile affections: for even their women did change the natural use into that which is against nature: And likewise also the men, leaving the natural use of the woman, burned in their lust one toward another; men with men working that which is unseemly, and receiving in themselves that recompence of their error which was met.

30 1 Corinthians 6:9-11: Know that the unrighteous shall not inherit the kingdom of God? Be not deceived: neither fornicators, nor idolaters, nor adulterers, nor effeminate, nor abusers of themselves with mankind, Nor thieves, nor covetous, nor drunkards, nor revilers, nor extortioners, shall inherit the kingdom of God. And such were some of you: but you are washed, but you are sanctified, but you are justified in the name of the Lord Jesus, and by the Spirit of our God.

31 1 Timothy 1:8-11: But we know that the law is good, if a man use it lawfully; Knowing this, that the law is not made for a righteous man, but for the lawless and disobedient, for the ungodly and for sinners, for unholy and profane, for murderers of fathers and murderers of mothers, for manslayers, For whoremongers, for them that defile

guidance (for example, the case of homosexual mob rape in Genesis 19, [32] and Judges 19, [33] or the commentary on these in the letter of Jude [34] . [35]

These five texts are uniformly negative regarding the behavior they address. The question is: *what are the texts referring to?* I did extensive study to understand the historical context of Leviticus and the Pauline letters. This is important work because the meaning of any given text is rooted in its original historical context.

Reading the Text in Historical Context

Let's pause to consider this important aspect of interpreting Scripture. Understanding the historical context is essential in order to draw reasonable conclusions from words composed in vastly different settings than our own. As John Walton, author and professor of Old Testament at Wheaton College, succinctly explains:

---

themselves with mankind, for menstealers, for liars, for perjured persons, and if there be any other thing that is contrary to sound doctrine; According to the glorious gospel of the blessed God, which was committed to my trust.

32 Genesis 19:4-5 But before they lay down, the men of the city, even the men of Sodom, compassed the house round, both old and young, all the people from every quarter: And they called unto Lot, and said unto him, Where are the men which came in to you this night? bring them out unto us, that we may know them.

33 Judges 19:22 Now as they were making their hearts merry, behold, the men of the city, certain sons of Belial, beset the house round about, and beat at the door, and spoke to the master of the house, the old man, saying, Bring forth the man that came into your house, that we may know him.

34 Jude 1:7 Even as Sodom and Gomorrah, and the cities about them in like manner, giving themselves over to fornication, and going after strange flesh, are set forth for an example, suffering the vengeance of eternal fire).

35 Hays, *Moral Vision*, p. 381

We believe the Bible was written for us, that it's for everyone of all times and places because it's God's Word. But it wasn't written to us. It wasn't written in our language, it wasn't written with our culture in mind or our culture in view. Therefore, if we want to get the best benefit from the communication, we need to try to enter their world, hear it as the audience would have heard it and as the author would have meant it, and read it in those terms. [36]

Walton speaks of Scripture as a "context rich" form of communication. In other words, the biblical writers were speaking to those who shared a rich cultural context, which shaped the way they communicated. I grew up in Detroit and share a rich cultural context with other Detroiters. When I say words like lions, tigers, and wings, I don't have to specify that I mean the professional football, baseball, and hockey teams. Fellow Detroiters get it because we share a rich cultural context.

Whether a communication is ambiguous or not is affected by this shared context. If we know the context well, we are much less likely to ask, "What *exactly* did you mean by that?" We know what our concerns are and we infer that the person communicating with us is addressing those particular concerns. If I say to some kids roughhousing in church, "Don't kill anyone," they know what concern I am addressing. They know I'm exaggerating for emphasis and not speaking in general terms—that I'm not, for example, commenting on the morality of military service. Stripped of the rich context we share, the mere words, "Don't kill anyone" could easily be understood to mean don't kill *anyone, anytime, ever.*

Reading text, including Scripture, means reading context. The text itself doesn't always provide the kind of background information that establishes the cultural context for those who

---

36 *Understanding Genesis with John Walton: http://biologos.org/ resources/multimedia/john-walton-on-understanding-genesis*

don't understand it by living in it. For that we have to rely on other historical sources that shed light on the context.

In the last century and a half, there has been an explosion of new data that sheds light on the historical context of Scripture. In one lecture I attended, John Walton said that for the first few centuries, the early church had access to one extra-biblical source to provide a sense of the historical context of the most ancient writings of Scripture. Today, he said, there are about a million such sources. When I asked when these sources were discovered, he described a surge of discovery beginning around 1850, when "people started digging around in that part of the world."

Works are being discovered that shed new light, better translations of those works are being developed, and all this new information is making its way from the academic settings that specialize in such things, to the biblical scholars who depend on this information to do their work. This work of biblical scholarship takes even more time to inform pastors and others who try to keep up with this stuff because they have the time and inclination to do so. No wonder so many people are checking their assumptions about what various Scripture texts actually mean in light of new information available about the historical context in which they were written. This is an exciting and vibrant time to better understand what the Bible actually means when it says something!

It turns out that historical context matters a lot when it comes to understanding texts having to do with sex and gender. Communication about *anything* having to do with sex would certainly be "context rich:" the meaning of such communication would depend a great deal on understanding the historical context.

For example, the category "homosexual," associated as it is with a predominant same-sex attraction or "sexual orientation," was unknown in the biblical period. In fact, it's a relatively recent understanding, judging by the late arrival of the term "homosexuality" in English. [37] This doesn't mean people were necessarily unaware of those who were sexually attracted to members of the same gender. But it does mean the phenomenon wasn't treated with nearly the recognition, significance, or understanding that we have today. At the very least, it means that people thought differently about what two men having sex meant. This isn't a particularly controversial finding among the scholars—most everyone agrees that it is so. But I didn't know this, until I took it upon myself to study the matter more deeply.

Men in the period in which the Pauline texts were written viewed male beauty as the higher and more aesthetically pleasing form of human beauty. Such a thought never even occurred to me. Furthermore, a man's having sex was viewed as a sign of his strength, and strength was viewed as a form of male virtue. The word "virtue" is related to the word "virility." Male penetration, often violent and having no association with love, was celebrated in society as a display of masculine strength. Representations of the phallus were openly displayed and celebrated.

Even married men engaged in penalty-free sex with slaves, concubines and underage males. Slavery was endemic and sexual services were expected. It is virtually certain that many more men were having sex with other males, including boys, than is the case today, and that most of these men were not "homosexual" in the sense that we use the term today.

Comparatively little is known about the extent or practice of lesbian sex during that period.

These are not minor differences between the biblical period and our own. These are *major and important* differences between the biblical period and our own. [38] And I was barely

---

37 Coined in the late 19th century, see: http://plato.stanford.edu/entries/homosexuality/

38 This is well attested in several sources. Especially helpful is: Ruden, Sarah. *Paul Among the People*. New York, N.Y.: Random House Inc, 2008; p 5, pp 45-71. Cantarella, Eva. *Bisexuality in the Ancient World*.

aware of these differences—no, I was completely ignorant of them—until I did my homework. I felt chastened by my ignorance. It was humbling to realize that I told people that the Bible clearly and unambiguously condemned all same-sex intimacy without considering this pertinent historical background, *because I hadn't done my homework.* Suffice it to say I felt a need to interpret and, even more, to apply the texts with corresponding caution.

I will now present a reading of the prohibitive texts that highlights the difficulties in treating the biblical prohibitions as a sweeping condemnation of all same-sex relationships today. I think it adds up to a reasonable possibility that the texts are not addressing the morality of what happens between same-sex couples who love each other as equals and express their sexuality in the context of a loving, monogamous relationship.

Regarding such texts as clearly prohibiting all such relationships is commonly asserted. [39] I won't summarize the arguments for this view because it has been done exhaustively elsewhere. The effect of this traditional reading is thoroughgoing exclusion of all gay persons from the life and ministry of the church, which is widely practiced. [40] This reading has the support of many faithful Christians, so it is by definition weighty. It may be correct. But it is *not* indisputably

---

New Haven and London: Yale University Press, 2002. An earlier source is: Boswell, John. *Christianity, Social Tolerance, and Homosexuality: Gay People in Western Europe from the Beginning of the Christian Era to the Fourteenth Century.* Chicago and London: The University of Chicago Press, 1980.

39 See Gagnon, Robert A. J. *The Bible and Homosexual Practice.* Nashville, Tenn.: Abingdon Press, 2001.

40 Gagnon argues for exclusion from church membership at least for those churches that exclude for unrepentant incest, polygamy, adultery, prostitution and fornication, Gagnon, *The Bible and Homosexual Practice,* pp. 489-490.

correct, as is often assumed. After close examination, I found *big* problems with this reading of the texts.

The Leviticus Abomination

The first prohibition is found in the book of Leviticus. "Thou shalt not lie with mankind, as with womankind: it is abomination." (Leviticus 18:22) "If a man also lie with mankind, as he lieth with a woman, both of them have committed an abomination: they shall surely be put to death; their blood shall be upon them." (Leviticus 20:13) This portion of Scripture is part of the block of laws referred to as the Holiness Code. It states that a man must not "lie with a man as with a woman." Leviticus has nothing to say about lesbian sex. [41] "Lie with" is generally thought to be a euphemism for anal intercourse. Philo, a Jewish commentator and contemporary of Jesus and Paul, understood this as a reference to male temple prostitution. [42] Male shrine prostitutes are mentioned several times in the Old Testament. [43] Robert Gagnon, a conservative scholar who argues for the traditional view, notes that Leviticus 18 was produced with homosexual cult prostitution in view, given the context of Canaanite and Egyptian idolatry. [44]

While Leviticus 18 uses the term "abomination" to refer to a man lying with another man, the Hebrew term, *toevah*, translated "abomination" or "detestable," is used to describe foods that may not be eaten (see Deuteronomy/Devarim 14:3, Orthodox Jewish Bible). In English, "abomination" implies

---

41 Commenting on Leviticus 18, Hays says, "Nothing is said here about female homosexual behavior." *Moral Vision*, p. 381.

42 Philo, *The Special Laws*, III, VII, 40-42 (40)

43 See Deuteronomy 23:17-18; 1 Kings 14:24; 15:12; 2 Kings.23:7

44 Gagnon in *The Bible and Homosexual Practice* states on p 130, "I do not doubt that the circles out of which Leviticus 18:22 was produced had in view homosexual cult prostitution, at least partly. Homosexual cult prostitution appears to have been the primary form in which homosexual intercourse was practiced in Israel."

severe condemnation reserved for the most egregious forms of immorality; this doesn't seem to be consistent with the dietary uses of *toevah*. The attempt to resolve this by categorizing one as a matter of moral concern and the other as a matter of ritual purity is not easy to establish on the basis of textual evidence. [45]

The Shameful Lust of Romans

The most extensive treatment of homosexual practice is found in Paul's letter to the Romans. The text in question reads, "Wherefore God also gave them up to uncleanness through the lusts of their own hearts, to dishonour their own bodies between themselves: Who changed the truth of God into a lie, and worshipped and served the creature more than the Creator, who is blessed for ever. Amen. For this cause God gave them up unto vile affections: for even their women did change the natural use into that which is against nature: And likewise also the men, leaving the natural use of the woman, burned in their lust one toward another; men with men working that which is unseemly, and receiving in themselves that recompense of their error which was meet." (Romans 1:24-27).

Like Leviticus 18, Romans 1 is framed as commentary on pagan idolatry. The practices referenced are, in fact cited as the *effect* of end-stage paganism. God is said to have "given over" the pagan idolaters to such behavior because of persistent and egregious idolatry. [46] The pagan idolaters of Romans 1:24-27 are "inflamed with lust"—a particularly intense form of unrestrained passion. This is followed by a list of vices that Luke Timothy Johnson calls "cold hearted vices"— the sins of the overtly and insolently rebellious. [47]

---

45 Hays, *Moral Vision*, p. 382

46 *Ibid.*, p 385, p. 388.

47 Johnson, Luke Timothy. *Reading Romans: A Literary and Theological Commentary*. Macon, Ga.: Smyth and Helwys, 2012.

Given that each text of Scripture must be read in historical context—the meaning of the text cannot be divorced from the what the text would have communicated to Roman Christians of the first century—the link between sexual practice and Gentile idolatry is central, not incidental, to Paul's argument. It's important to realize that this context is foreign to most of us, bizarre even. The Greco-Roman gods were viewed as sexual beings. Zeus practiced pederastic sex (more about that later) with Ganymede, a young male god. [48] The practice of temple prostitution (temple prostitutes servicing clients in the context of pagan worship) linked sexual perversion with idolatry, the historical context of Romans 1.

It is reasonable to think that the original recipients of Paul's letter, all too familiar with the widespread practices of temple prostitution, would have viewed this first and foremost as a condemnation of such practices. That's not to say other same-sex practices would have been excluded, necessarily, just that this would have been front and center in the minds of the original hearers. (Remember, Paul's letter would have been heard, not read, by most people.)

Most modern readers, at least in the developed world, are completely unfamiliar with temple prostitution. Temple prostitution is the last thing modern readers imagine when they hear of homoerotic sex; most of us imagine modern versions of homosexual relationships. But these modern versions are very different than the things the Roman Christians were familiar with. And temple prostitution is just one example.

The Greco-Roman world was rife with a practice, unknown to us moderns, called pederasty. Pederasty refers to a widespread practice in Roman society in which men took young men and boys (pre-pubescent minors) under their wing as mentors. The older men provided the young males access to privileges that only elders had access to in exchange for

48 Buxton, Richard. *The Complete World of Greek Mythology*. New York, N.Y.: Thames and Hudson, 2004. p 100.

sexual services. The older men weren't interested in "gay sex" in the way that we think of it. Most of them were attracted to young, pre-pubescent males, who, relative to older males, had feminine qualities. The sexual penetration was violent and degrading. The younger partner (we would say victim) felt demeaned by it and it was thought to "feminize" him.

Remember, male beauty was the highest form of human physical beauty in the ancient world (the opposite of our modern tendency to associate "beauty" with females). Were some of the older men who practiced pederasty what we would call "same-sex attracted"? Probably, but the vast majority would have been what we call straight. As noted earlier, any comparison between the modern world and the ancient world is very difficult because "homosexuality," in the sense we use it today (people who are primarily sexually attracted to members of the same sex), wasn't a recognized category.

Today, pederasts would be treated as criminals for the sexual exploitation of vulnerable boys. They would be charged with rape and imprisoned for a very long time. But in that time, pederasty was a socially accepted arrangement, an institution of Greco-Roman society. It was widespread. Many parents of young males, especially those who had some privilege in Roman society, would not want their sons to participate in this arrangement. But it was far from criminalized. And, like virtually every other institution in Greco-Roman society, pederasty was linked to pagan idolatry.

This raises an important question of interpretation. Is the text a sweeping condemnation of all same-sex practice or does it speak to the *predominant* practices of the time, especially temple prostitution and pederasty?

But there's yet another form of homoerotic sex that would have been very widespread in Roman society and well known to the recipients of Paul's letter: the sexual services that masters demanded of their slaves.

In a telling aside, the highly respected commentator Robert Jewett, who seems to support the traditional view on homosexuality, says:

> *It remains puzzling why Paul assumes that his audience, consisting of a majority coming from a background in which same-sex relations were often tolerated, would have accepted Paul's point of view without argument. While the Jewish background of Paul's heterosexual preference has been frequently cited as decisive by previous researchers, little attention has been given to the correlation between homosexuality and slavery. The right of masters to demand sexual services from slaves and freedmen is an important factor in grasping the impact of Paul's rhetoric, because slavery was so prominent a feature of the social background of most of Paul's audience in Rome.* [49]

In other words, we have three very significant and pervasive sexual practices that would have been well known to Paul's audience and would shape their view of same-gender sexual practices: temple prostitution, pederasty, and the sexual services required of slaves. Yet, these same practices are virtually unknown to many modern readers. You'd have to be a history buff to know of them. To others, they are merely a historical footnote that has little impact on the imagination as we read his words today. [50] But how would we modern readers understand Paul's condemnation of same-sex practice if widespread and widely accepted institutions like temple

49 Jewett, Robert. *Romans: A Commentary*. Minneapolis, Minn.: Fortress Press, 2007. p. 180.

50 I was surprised to see that in what was otherwise a thoughtful treatment of homosexuality in *A Moral Vision of the New Testament*, Richard Hays does not even address the possibility that Paul may have these practices in view in Romans 1, which is explicitly about pagan idolatry.

prostitution, pederasty, and slavery had shaped our view of it? When reading Romans 1, would we think of two men or two women who have formed their own family unit, having made commitments to each other, and are now raising children together? Arguably not.

This latter point, of course, is hotly disputed. In my study of this debate I found two examples cited to support the notion that the historical context of Romans certainly includes the condemnation of what is analogous to today's monogamous gay unions—loving relationships between equal partners who are "homosexual" in the modern sense that they are strongly, perhaps exclusively, attracted to members of the same sex.

One commentator, N.T. Wright (an imposing and brilliant figure in New Testament scholarship), cites the "marriage" of the emperor Nero to a young male named Sporus as evidence that Paul's understanding of homosexuality was not unlike our own. [51] The implication is that Paul would certainly have something analogous to today's monogamous gay unions in mind in his condemnations. However, Nero eyed Sporus, then a male child by today's standards, had him castrated, dressed him as a woman and referred to him as his "wife." [52] This hardly seems equivalent to any of the gay partnerships I know.

Sometimes Plato's Symposium is cited as clear evidence that Paul would surely have known of the ancient equivalent to modern same-sex monogamous relationships. [53]

By inference, at least, it is further asserted by Wright and others that the text includes such relationships in its condemnation. However, when I dusted off my (unread) copy of Plato's Symposium, the section in question amounts to a defense of an idealized form of pederasty in which the youth seduced by the older mentor wants the relationship for the

51 Wright, N.T. *Paul for Everyone: Romans Part 1.* Louisville, Ky.: Westminster John Knox Press, 2004. 22.

52 Vout, Caroline. *Power and Eroticism in Imperial Rome.* Cambridge: Cambridge University Press (2007), 152.

53 N.T. Wright, among others, asserts this.

right reasons and the mentor has "noble" reasons as well. [54]
How this is anything like modern-day monogamous same-sex
relationships is beyond me.

Sarah Ruden, a Greco-Roman scholar steeped in this
literature more than any New Testament scholar, debunks the
idea that Plato knew of gay relationships that are equivalent
to today's monogamous gay unions, formed as co-equal
partnerships between adults who are committed to lifelong
fidelity. [55] This says nothing of the fact that Plato was writing
some 400 years before the New Testament era. In other words,
Wright's contention is highly disputed, and not without
evidence by reputable scholars.

Yes, given the prevalence of pederasty it is possible, likely
even, that at least some continued their sexual relationship
well into the adulthood of the minor party. But this can hardly
be regarded as anything but exploitative. Furthermore, Ruden
demonstrates how the passive partner in homoerotic sex
would have been treated. It is nothing other than exploitative.
Reading her sources is not for the faint of heart.

The fact is, when scholars search the literature of the
period, they can find untold examples of same-sex acts in
the context of pederasty, temple prostitution, and slavery.
The case for asserting the existence of something like
contemporary monogamous gay unions is sketchy at best.
To assert with great confidence that such relationships were
well known to Paul doesn't seem justified. Even if there were

---

54 See the speech of Pausanias, pp. 534-538, *Plato: The Collected
Dialogues*, Edited by Edith Hamilton and Huntington Cairns,
Princeton University Press.

55 See Ruden, *Paul Among the People*, chapter 3, especially: "Readers
may think that I am exaggerating, that the day to day culture of
homosexuality could not have been so bad. They may have heard of
Platonic homoerotic sublimity or festive or friendly couplings. None
of the sources, objectively read, backs any of this up." See also, her
discussion of the relevant dialogue in Plato's Symposium, beginning on
p. 58.

relationships that were closer to contemporary monogamous gay partnerships, is this what Romans is addressing when it speaks as it does? I think it's much more likely that Paul's argument—never intended as a pastoral guide for individuals, per se—is offered in a shared context dominated by same-sex acts characteristic of pederasty, temple prostitution, and slave sex, which were grossly perverse, demeaning, and exploitative.

A final consideration—a nagging question of interpretation—means a great deal to me as a pastor who has come to know lesbian couples, some of whom are raising children together. When read in historical context, the text is arguably ambiguous regarding women. Most of the commentators I consulted, including Robert Jewett, whose commentary in the *Hermeneia* series is widely regarded as the most exhaustive, suppose that Paul is speaking of lesbian sex here. But most also admit that the nature of such relationships is not known, since there is so little attention paid to such liaisons in the literature of the period. Cantarella indicates that Greek society separated the sexes for initiation where girls sometimes had sex with adult females. [56] How widespread this practice was, seems unknown.

Most commentators at least note the difficulty in understanding what Paul is referring to because the language used is not as explicit in the case of women as it is in the case of men: "their women exchanged natural relations for unnatural" is more ambiguous than "men committed shameful acts with other men." Which form of "unnatural relations" is Paul referring to? If you are a gay woman who is partnered with another woman and the two of you are raising children together, a great deal hinges on the answer to that

---

56 Cantarella, Eva. *Bisexuality in the Ancient World*. New Haven and London: Yale University Press, 2002. p. 83: "Sex during initiation, for boys, was with an adult. For girls, on the other hand, it was sometimes with their mistresses, and sometimes ... with another girl of the same age."

question. As a pastor caring for these women, a great deal hinges on my answer to that question.

On balance, I'd have to agree: Paul may well have some form of lesbian sex in view. Paul is certainly not taking pains to distinguish the case of men from the case of women. But this is not a "slam dunk" conclusion. I'm still arguing with myself and with some friends over this one.

I wonder: if Romans has Leviticus 18-20 in the background (both are commentary on the pagan practices associated with idolatry) the "unnatural relations" involving women could be an allusion to bestiality. Bestiality, and not lesbian sex, is the perversion of women that parallels a "man lying with a man" in Leviticus 18 and 20, where both are mentioned. [57]

Since the language with respect to the "unnatural relations" of women isn't explicit, others have posited that Paul may have had anal or femoral intercourse in view. [58] There is evidence that the revered church fathers, Augustine and Anastasius, may have thought it referred to a form of "unnatural" sexual relations other than lesbianism. [59] If the rites of female initiation included sex between a girl and an adult mistress, one can imagine this as an abhorrent practice to Paul and thus his primary referent.

This would all be much less of a concern were there *any other reference at all* to lesbian sex in the entire Bible, but there is not.

---

57 In support of this view, Paul's only Bible was the Old Testament, and Romans, chapter one can be seen as his version of the holiness code of Leviticus 18-20, both of which are framed around the behavior of the people of God as distinct from the surrounding pagan society.

58 Ruden, *Paul Among the People*

59 Brooten, Bernadette. *"Patristic Interpretations of Romans 1:26."* Studia Patristica XVIII: Papers of the 1983 Oxford Patristics Conference. Ed. Elizabeth Livingstone.(1985): 338-340. The Writings of St. Paul: Annotated Texts, Reception and Criticism. 2d ed. vol. 1 Ed. Wayne A. Meeks and John T. Fitzgerald. New York: Norton, 2007, p. 287.

Let me just pause here for a moment and let you into my dilemma. I cited N.T. Wright as a scholar who thinks Paul would ban the equivalent of modern-day gay unions. I cannot overestimate how highly I regard the scholarship of N.T. Wright. His writings have had a huge influence on my understanding of the gospel, have helped me to know Jesus better. He's among a handful of scholars that I regard as theological heroes. Disagreeing with Wright gives *me* pause. A member of my congregation said, "Ken, you are out on a limb here. Do you expect me to agree with you over against N.T. Wright?" I said, "I certainly don't. If I were you, I wouldn't." But that's just it. I'm not just a member of my congregation. I'm a pastor who has the responsibility to advise two women who are committed to each other and their children on whether the Bible condemns the sexual dimension of their relationship. I don't find N.T. Wright's assertion convincing. And I cannot outsource my pastoral responsibility to N.T. Wright.

In a situation like this, a *pastor* is left to make the call. Am I to use this text to guide my care of the people I know who are in what appear to be loving, caring relationships involving same-sex intimacy? The text, in my view, is certainly not *aimed* at them. I feel confident to say that this text is speaking to the kind of wicked behavior—to speak of "relationships" would be completely inapt—to which an idolatrous society is given over as sign that it has fallen under the judgment of God. This, in my judgment, fits the sexual practices that characterize awful institutions like pederasty, or temple prostitution, or the horrible way slave masters use the bodies of people they think they *own*. It does *not* fit the relationships of the same-sex couples I know.

This level of detail is difficult to fit into a thirty-five minute sermon. If you've made it through the dizzying array of details that I have presented after engaging in a lengthy—years long—study consulting several commentaries and reading several books for historical background, you are a highly motivated reader. And your eyes are glazing over. But this level of detail is absolutely necessary to speak as a pastor with any informed confidence to a gay person.

As a pastor, I didn't need help to discern how to respond to temple prostitution, pederasty, and slave sex. I was dealing with gay people who had strong same-sex attraction from childhood—some from devout Christian homes—who endured a period of deep anguish about their sexuality, perhaps sought healing to no avail, and were tempted to suicide. After much soul searching, some had come to believe that they were called to a faithful covenantal relationship with a same-sex partner. Others came to the church with pre-existing commitments of this sort, and some were parents with kids in tow.

Even traditional commentators agree that Romans 1 is not to be used as a condemnation of specific individuals. [60] Richard Hays goes so far as to say, "The aim of Romans 1 is not to teach a code of sexual ethics; nor is the passage a warning of God's judgment against those who are guilty of particular sins." [61] Thus, the text does not offer either a pastoral approach or a church policy regarding the people involved. In fact, the exhortation that flows from Romans is to condemn those who would judge others, while participating in any of a wide range of other sins! [62]

When I consulted more conservative or traditional sources—highly regarded sources—I found them unconvincing. And this, in particular, was telling: *they simply weren't dealing with the questions that I faced as a pastor.*

---

60 For example, "To use these texts appropriately in ethical reflection about homosexuality, we should not try to wring rules out of them, nor should we abstract principles from them." Hays, *Moral Vision*, p. 396.

61 *Ibid.*, p. 387.

62 Romans 2:1 Therefore you are inexcusable, O man, whosoever you are that judges: for when you judge another, you condemn yourself; for you that judges doest the same things. Stowers, Stanley K. *A Rereading of Romans* (New Haven, London: Yale University Press, 1994. p. 12.

Many traditional commentators are now reluctant to describe same-sex orientation with terms like "shameful lust," or "vile affections" found in Romans. Yet, the same commentators insist on applying the prohibition of Romans to all same-sex relationships, including modern monogamous gay unions. It seems to me that with a fair reading of the text, one can't have it both ways. If the text applies to all modern-day gay unions, then all of the text applies, including the part of the text that characterizes the orientation (i.e. the desire for the activity) as deeply shameful, abhorrent, perverse.

As a case in point, the conservative commentator Hendrickson, echoing many others, says that "A person's sexual orientation, whether heterosexual or homosexual is not the point at issue. What matters is what a person does with his sexuality!" [63]   But in Romans 1, Paul says that "God gave them over to shameful lusts" as a punishment for their end-stage paganism. The acts are not disconnected from the shameful lusts that precede them. Hendrickson's clear distinction between orientation and behavior may be a helpful pastoral distinction, but it does not seem to be derived from the text at all—quite the contrary. Yet, Paul's framing, applied to all same-sex relationships, is in stark contrast to the experience of so many. Is God in the business, for example, of giving over children in Christian families to their shameful lusts as a punishment for gross idolatry? Or, to make it more indirect, are the children in these families the unfortunate, if innocent, manifestation of a society that has been given over to shameful lusts as a punishment for gross and persistent idolatry? Are we willing to live with a reading of the text that results in viewing God in this way? I am not.

The limitations and difficulties of Romans 1 are significant, because the remaining New Testament texts are even more problematic as guides in the care of gay couples. Get ready for

---

63 Hendriksen, W., & Kistemaker, S. J. *New Testament Commentary Vol. 12-13: Exposition of Paul's Epistle to the Romans*. Grand Rapids, Mich.: Baker Book House, 1953-2001.

some more mind-numbing detail that doesn't make for snappy, easy-to-digest sermons.

1 Corinthians and 1 Timothy: Effeminate? Male Prostitutes? Homosexual Offender?

The next occurrence is Paul's letter to the Corinthians: *Do you know that the unrighteous shall not inherit the kingdom of God? Do not be not deceived: neither fornicators, nor idolaters, nor adulterers, nor effeminate, nor abusers of themselves with mankind (1 Corinthians 6:9).*

Two Greek terms, *malakoi* (KJV, "effeminate") and *arsenokoitai* (KJV "abusers of themselves with mankind"), appear in a list of vices. Vice lists, by definition, are not useful to define the behaviors in view when the precise meaning of terms is uncertain. [64] This is especially the case when Scripture doesn't treat the behaviors indicated in more depth elsewhere. For example, the mere listing of adultery in a vice list doesn't help us understand whether remarriage after divorce or lusting after a woman constitutes adultery. For that we need more than a vice list and Scripture provides it, offering many specific examples of adultery. These relevant examples are missing with respect to same-sex relationships. In fact, there is not a single condemnation in scripture that is specifically and explicitly aimed at monogamous gay couples.

The Greek terms employed by Paul in 1 Corinthians 6:9, *malakoi* and *arsenokoitai*, are notoriously difficult to translate. [65] Martin Luther translates *malakoi* as "*weichlinge*" or

---

64 "The proper way to read such lists is not to dwell so much on their individual elements as to assess their overall impact. Such lists were based on the premise that wicked people tended to practice all the vices, just as good people practiced all the virtues." Johnson, *Reading Romans.*

65 Soards, Marion. L. *Scripture and Homosexuality, Biblical Authority and the Church Today* (Louisville, Ky.: Westminster John Knox Press, 1995) p 18-20. Fee, Gordon. D. *The First Epistle to the Corinthians, The*

"weaklings" [66] and *arsenokoitai* as "*knabenschänder*," a German word that means "ravisher of male youth." [67] Neither term is connected in any way to monogamous gay relationships.

The first term, *malakoi*, has also been rendered "effeminate" (KJV), "male prostitutes" (NIV), "weakling" (Luther, 1522), [68] "catamites" (handsome young men kept for sexual purposes, analogous to Ganymede, the young consort of Zeus). [69]

I was particularly affected by Gordon Fee's commentary on 1 Corinthians 6:9. I've met Fee, loved his books, and trust him as a man of the Spirit and a man of the Book. So it catches my attention when Fee candidly elaborates on the translation difficulties over these two key Greek words. Fee writes, "The first word, *malakoi*, has the basic meaning of 'soft' but it also came to mean 'effeminate,' most likely referring to the younger, 'passive' partner in a pederastic relationship—a common form of homosexuality in the Greco-Roman world. In many instances, young men sold themselves as 'mistresses' for the sexual pleasure of men older than themselves. The problem is that there was a technical word for such men, and *malakos* is seldom, if ever, so used. *Since it is not the ordinary word for homosexual behavior, one cannot be sure what it means in*

New International Commentary on the New Testament. Grand Rapids, Mich.: William B. Eerdmans Publishing Co., 1987; p. 244.

66 Jung, *Heterosexism: An Ethical Challenge.* In 1522 Martin Luther translated this term Weichlinge or "weaklings"

67 Switzer, David K. *Pastoral Care of Gays, Lesbians and Their Families.* Minneapolis, Minn.: Augsburg Fortress, 1999: Luther, in his translation of the New Testament published in 1522, used the word *Knabenschänder* to translate the word *arsenokoitai* both in 1 Corinthians and 1 Timothy. This German word means raper or ravisher of male youth. Luther knew on the basis of his research that the Greek word was not to be used to refer to all homosexual acts, but only to one type, the pederast.

68 Jung, Patricia Beattie. *Heterosexism: An Ethical Challenge.* Albany, N.Y.: State University of New York Press, 1993.

69 Buxton, *The Complete World of Greek Mythology.* p 100

a list like this, where there is no further context to help [italics added]." [70] Fee suggests that *malakoi* means "male prostitute" or "effeminate call boy" but adds that this is only a "best guess."
[71]

The next term, *arsenokoitai,* is even more problematic. Fee says, "This word (*arsenokoitai*), however, is also difficult. This is the first appearance in preserved literature, and subsequent authors are reluctant to use it, especially when describing homosexual activity." [72] Fee notes that the word is a compound with roots meaning "male" and "intercourse" but adds, "what is not certain is whether 'male' is subject ('males who have intercourse'; thus a word for male prostitutes of all kinds) or object ('intercourse with males' therefore male homosexual)." [73]

I could see for myself the difficulty in understanding what the term refers to by comparing the different English translations: "sodomites" (NRSV), "homosexual offenders" (NIV), "homosexuals" (NASB), "abusers of themselves with mankind" (KJV) and "child molesters" (Martin Luther).

To summarize: Fee regards "effeminate call boy" for *malakoi* as "a best guess" and NIV's "homosexual offender" (itself an ambiguous term) for *arsenokoitai* as only "very likely moving toward a proper understanding." [74]

But, wait a minute. Any translation that uses the modern term "homosexual"—common in modern translations—is seriously misleading for two reasons. First, it obscures the fact that only men are in view, since the term in Greek only applies to men. Second, the use of "homosexual" in translation obscures the fact that homosexuality was not a category in use in the biblical period. As is attested by many sources, the *predominant* same-sex practices of the Greco-Roman world were very different than the practices debated within the

---

70 Fee, *The First Epistle to the Corinthians*, p. 244.

71 *Ibid.*, p. 244.

72 *Ibid.*, p 244

73 *Ibid.*, p. 244.

74 *Ibid.*, p 244

church today. [75] Is that the best we can do, given all the above
ambiguities?

The plural of *arsenokoitai* (*aresenokoitais)* appears in
1 Timothy 1:10: "for whoremongers, for them that defile
themselves with mankind, for menstealers, for liars, for
perjured persons, and if there be any other thing that is
contrary to sound doctrine." This term (KJV "them that defile
themselves with mankind") also appears in a vice list and
offers no further clues to its meaning. [76] The term *malakoi* is
noticeably absent.

The Questions Raised Are Legitimate

In short, my study affirmed my pastoral instinct that
whatever the Bible was addressing seemed to have a different
context, tone, and application than fit the people I was
thinking about. In the abstract, it's easier to gloss over the
significant questions raised by a closer look at the texts. But
I was now well beyond that. My questions seemed both
legitimate and significant. These were not your typical "How
can we find a way to ignore what the Bible says?" questions.
No, I concluded that there are real problems in applying the
prohibitions of Leviticus 18, 20; Romans 1; 1 Corinthians
6; and 1 Timothy 1 to people in modern monogamous
gay unions. When a scholar of Fee's stature describes the
difficulties in translating *malakoi* and *arsenokoitai,* a pastor
has good reason to exercise caution before excluding same-sex
couples on the grounds that these texts speak clearly. In this
case, the exegetical uncertainty is far from insignificant.

I'd like to stress some of the challenges I faced in my study.
No single author did my homework for me. I couldn't find a
single commentary or topical treatment of homosexuality that
addressed the concerns I had. I found that most conservative
scholarly commentators did not draw my attention to the

---

75 Ruden, *Paul Among the People*, p. 45-71.

76 "The context offers little discussion of sexual morality as such."
Hays, *Moral Vision*, p. 383.

range of legitimate exegetical concerns in other pertinent
texts. For example, J.R. Daniel Kirk, assistant professor of
New Testament at Fuller Theological Seminary, recently
upheld the traditional view but expressed some openness to
reconsidering it. [77] Yet, even Kirk fails to note the prominence
of temple prostitution, pederasty, and slave sex in the Greco-
Roman context. Hays' careful and thoughtful chapter on
homosexuality was marked by the same omission. [78]

Most conservative scholars didn't comment on the pastoral
implications of the exegetical [79] issues. They simply did not
seem to be engaged with the pastoral concerns that I had. [80] I
have great respect for InterVarsity Christian Fellowship, but in
the IVP Academic commentary on Romans by Grant Osborne,
the biblical teaching against homosexuality was summarized
as follows: "The Old Testament contains many condemnations
of homosexual practices (Genesis 19:5, 8; Leviticus 18:22 and
20:13; Deuteronomy 23:17-18; Judges 19:22-24; 1 Kings 14:24
and 15:12; 2 Kings 23:7; Isaiah 1:9 and 3:9; Lamentations
4:6)." In the same section, Osborne asserts that Scripture
condemns all same-sex activity. He does this without making
any distinctions among the various practices. Yet Osborne
neglects to point out that Genesis 19:5,8 and Judges 19:22-24
are references to attempted violent gang rape; that Isaiah 9 and
3:9 and Lamentations 4:6 simply reference the city of Sodom
for crimes that are not specified; and that Deuteronomy 23:17-
18, 1 Kings 14:24 and 15:12, 2 Kings 23:7 all refer to male
shrine prostitutes. The gay undergraduate student reading this

---

77 See his chapter, Homosexuality Under the Reign of Christ, in *Jesus
Have I Loved, But Paul?* J.R. Daniel Kirk. Grand Rapids, Mich.: Baker
Academic, 2011.

78 *Moral Vision*, Hays, pp. 379-403. Pederasty is mentioned in a
footnote.

79 "exegetical" refers to the discipline of determining the meaning of
the text

80 Osborne, Grant. R. *Romans (IVP New Testament Commentary)*
Downers Grove, Ill.: VP Academic, 2010. p. 57

commentary will either do his or her own homework to figure this out or will be left with an exaggerated sense of certainty regarding the meaning of these texts. [81]

As I reviewed some of the writings that treat homosexuality in a topical manner, I saw that they fell predictably into their respective camps. [82] Neither the "open and affirming" position nor the traditional exclusionary one satisfied my concerns. Liberal approaches seemed willing to dismiss some of my biblical concerns while conservative approaches failed to take my pastoral concerns into account. The latter, in particular, seemed to make assumptions about homosexuality that I couldn't square with my pastoral experience or my reading.

I had to do a great deal of my own homework, evaluating arguments on both sides while trying to tease out the underlying assumptions. I became convinced that there were no "ready made" positions to adopt. I got used to the idea that this issue will not be resolved by simple appeal to the current literature or by selecting either the settled affirming view or the settled exclusionary one.

I found myself saying to pastors with growing conviction, "This issue is not going to be settled for us in the academy. This is ours to deal with as best we can and we can no longer avoid our responsibility." There are, no doubt, better pastors to deal with it. But I am the pastor of the Vineyard Church of Ann Arbor. And I realized I had to face it squarely and deal with it, come what may.

---

81 By contrast, Osborne's comments on Romans 7:2-3, in which Paul speaks of remarriage as illicit except after the death of a spouse shows more care for the pastoral considerations of the divorced and remarried, see p. 168-169.

82 Typical of these was: Via, Dan O. and Gagnon, Robert, A. J. *Homosexuality and the Bible: Two Views.* Minneapolis, Minn.: Fortress Press, 2003.

What the Bible Clearly Condemns: Plenty to Agree On

Far from dismissing the prohibitive texts as mistaken or lacking divine inspiration, it is clear from the historical context that there were several widespread practices *crying out* for condemnation. These texts need to be affirmed in light of these practices! Let me list them:

- Temple prostitution
- Homosexual orgiastic practices associated with pagan worship
- Homosexual services for hire
- Requiring homosexual services from slaves or others
- Adults engaging in pederasty
- Homosexual gang rape

The biblical emphasis on steadfast love and fidelity justifies an expanded circle of prohibitions:

- Pornography
- Casual or recreational sex
- Promiscuity
- Acts exerting dominance over others

For someone who wants to love people and the Bible, seeing this was such a relief! There is so much to agree on regarding the proper application of the biblical prohibitions of same-gendered sexual acts. This matters a great deal and it is often completely unrecognized in the heat of controversy. It reveals just how out of proportion this controversy has become. In fact, a relatively narrow matter of interpretation and application is at issue. And it sits squarely in the lap of pastors, not controversialists: is the Bible addressing modern-day monogamous gay unions at all? If the answer to that question is unclear, how are we to apply the prohibitions to gay people who are willing to practice lifelong fidelity with a same-sex partner?

After a period of in-depth study, I had arrived at a conclusion that has only become firmer with time. My discomfort with an exclusionary policy was too much. I couldn't justify it enough to practice it. I couldn't implement it. My conscience wouldn't allow it. I had been talking openly with our pastoral team and board as my concerns grew. But now I had to state my conviction—a matter of conscience— clearly. We had to deal with this. During this period I thought, "Should I resign as a pastor? Is this something I can pursue without disturbing too many good people?" For better or worse, I decided to continue my exploration.

After seeing that the prohibitive texts were insufficiently clear to justify the traditional position, and especially not clear enough to exclude people over it, I had to engage another key question. This came up whenever I shared my concerns with friends and colleagues. Many hadn't studied the texts closely, but could imagine that legitimate questions of interpretation and application might emerge with closer study. But they justified the exclusionary approach for a different reason, rooted in a definition of marriage: "Biblical marriage is for one man and one woman. Sex beyond that is forbidden. Isn't that clear enough?"

I'm going to treat that question—with all its highly controversial implications—soon enough. But in order to move forward in my discernment process, especially given the growing problems I was seeing in the traditional consensus position, I needed some breathing room. And I am a pastor of a local congregation. That means, for me to have breathing room, I need to be part of a congregation that has breathing room to work this thing out. We need to step out from under the intense pressure of the cultural-religious-political controversy of our highly polarized day, and find a new way forward.

CHAPTER 4

The Third Way

A New Approach to Inclusion

I'M NOW READY to sketch out the makings of a third way, a new approach to inclusion. It's a way to fully include people who are gay, lesbian, and transgender in the life of the church, while recognizing that the church has not yet resolved the question of the morality of gay relationships. Instead of forcing a resolution on that question, it calls for regarding it as a "disputable matter"—something we can agree to disagree on. It doesn't require the members of the church community to affirm gay relationships. It asserts the gospel truth that our common life in Jesus doesn't depend on granting each other moral approval. But it clearly rejects exclusion in all its forms as an appropriate response to people who are gay, lesbian and transgender. We'll begin by facing the reality of exclusion.

Theories of the nature, the cause, and the broader social consequences of homosexuality make for interesting conversations. But exclusionary practices, despite recent efforts to soften the tone of the "love the sinner, hate the sin" approach, have a sharp edge that hurts. All pastoral care, including exclusion from membership or disqualification from ministry, is particular—is practiced within complex and diverse *local* church cultures. Paul's letters show him practicing moral theology and recommending exclusion, when he does, in such particularized contexts. This makes it more difficult to distill universal exclusionary policies from his writings, especially in challenging cases. But it does encourage us to honor the local particularities in matters of exclusion.

We know that exclusion is the most severe punishment in the New Testament. It is equivalent to capital punishment in the Old Testament. We are speaking, after all, of exclusion from the community in which Christ is explicitly welcomed. To be in Christ is to be in community.

There are only two specific cases of exclusion recorded in the New Testament. The first is the case of Ananias and Sapphira in Acts 5, struck down by God for holding back a part of the proceeds of the sale of their property (or perhaps for lying about it.) [83] The second is in 1 Corinthians 5, where Paul urges the exclusion of a church member who is having

---

83 Acts 5:1-10 But a certain man named Ananias, with Sapphira his wife, sold a possession, And kept back part of the price, his wife also being privy to it, and brought a certain part, and laid it at the apostles' feet. But Peter said, Ananias, why has Satan filled your heart to lie to the Holy Ghost, and to keep back part of the price of the land? Whiles it remained, was it not your own? And after it was sold, was it not in your own power? Why have you conceived this thing in your heart? You have not lied to men, but to God. And Ananias hearing these words fell down, and gave up the ghost: and great fear came on all them that heard these things. And the young men arose, wound him up, and carried him out, and buried him. And it was about the space of three hours after, when his wife, not knowing what was done, came in. And Peter answered unto her, Tell me whether you sold the land for so much? And she said, Yes, for so much. Then Peter said to her, How is it that you have agreed together to tempt the Spirit of the Lord? Behold, the feet of them which have buried your husband are at the door, and shall carry you out. Then fell she down straightway at his feet, and yielded up the ghost: and the young men came in, and found her dead, and, carrying her forth, buried her by her husband.

sex with his father's wife (and the church is proud!)—a scandal for pagans idolaters as well as Paul. [84]

For years, I didn't face the reality of exclusion head on. Many Vineyard churches have "Come as you are, you'll be loved!" as a motto. We are known as churches with a wide-open door, receiving people whom other churches might not welcome. I had a reflexive instinct to discount the significance of exclusion with thoughts like, "That's not a big issue around here. We're not excluding people left and right over this!"

But I was kidding myself.

Few people need to be excluded in any formal sense. Our church, like so many others, is deeply affected by the high fluidity of membership in American churches. For better or worse, when moral concerns are addressed pastorally, they are often "resolved" by people self-deporting into other congregations. We had a process for formal exclusion based on "unrepentant immorality" buried in our church by-laws, but we never had to use it. If an issue rose to the level of needing a pastoral intervention, the conversation either went well or it didn't. If it didn't, people simply left on their own accord.

Even more significantly, a church culture exerts a powerful selective influence on who does or doesn't get involved in the first place. There are many people, including entire categories of people, who may not feel welcome in a given

---

84 1 Corinthians 5:1-5 It is reported commonly that there is fornication among you, and such fornication as is not so much as named among the Gentiles, that one should have his father's wife. And you are puffed up, and have not rather mourned, that he that has done this deed might be taken away from among you. For I verily, as absent in body, but present in spirit, have judged already, as though I were present, concerning him that has so done this deed, In the name of our Lord Jesus Christ, when you are gathered together, and my spirit, with the power of our Lord Jesus Christ, To deliver such an one unto Satan for the destruction of the flesh, that the spirit may be saved in the day of the Lord Jesus.

church. I had seen this at work with scientists and others who regard modern science as a legitimate and trusted authority. Because we were an evangelical congregation, scientists simply assumed that we opposed evolution. Until I took steps to change that, we didn't see many scientists in our church. This informal "pre-exclusion" is probably the more powerful and widely exerted form in many churches. It is in my denomination. As the divorced and remarried don't seek communion at a Roman Catholic parish, gays and lesbians don't seek to participate in most evangelical churches. For years, this was the case for the Ann Arbor Vineyard and it tended to mask how "big a deal" the gay issue really was.

To appreciate how I've navigated this question in my local church, let me give you a little more background about our denomination, Vineyard. We've never had a focus on church discipline. We've never adopted the Reformed tradition that sees church discipline as one of the distinguishing marks of the true church. As a Regional Overseer in my denomination (not unlike a "Bishop"), I'd often hear of pastors concerned about the national organization exercising a heavy-handed authority (over questions like giving the required three percent of church income to the national office.) It always amused me, this concern. As a Regional Overseer, I was in a position to exercise some discipline over Vineyard churches. I used to comment, only half jokingly, that it takes a great deal to be disciplined in the Vineyard. Still, when it was necessary, I did it.

Compared to other church traditions, my denomination had not adopted formal policies on many moral issues of equal or greater concern. Partly as a response to my questioning the traditional view as I have, my denomination recently issued a statement on this issue. I think that singling this issue out—especially in the absence of any national policy on more significant issues like divorce and remarriage— stigmatizes gay people. Stigmatizing a vulnerable minority is something we should repent of, not something we should perpetuate.

Our local church has no formal policies on this or many other moral concerns. The policies we do have are related to insuring the safety of minors in our care, an appropriate emphasis. If we have a hair trigger on the exclusion gun, shouldn't it be aimed at those who are using their power to abuse someone who is in a weaker, more vulnerable position?

We certainly don't have exclusionary policies when it comes to *contested* moral issues. The New Testament takes a dim view of resorting to violence to overthrow tyrannical governments, yet we do not threaten those who advocate this with exclusion. We don't threaten to exclude those who use contraceptive methods or fertility treatments that many Christians consider morally unacceptable, even though the moral concern at stake is murder. Instead, we help people to engage such questions on a case-by-case basis, making the best discernments possible, informed by Scripture and examination of conscience. In short, we trust the Spirit to guide us. We are not alone in this world.

We tend to reserve exclusion in its various forms for the most clear-cut cases and for situations in which a person's behavior is causing noticeable harm to others.

In other words, we take an ad hoc approach to exclusion. We do so reluctantly, as a last resort, rarely, and by making holistic discernments rather than by implementing categorical exclusions based on formal policies. This is, for lack of a better word, our tradition. In most Vineyard churches, the decision to exclude is reserved for the senior pastor, sometimes in consultation with a church board. Formal proceedings, such as we see practiced in the Reformed tradition, are often not observed. If they are, they are certainly not a well-developed strength of most Vineyard churches, including our own.

This approach has advantages and disadvantages. We depend heavily on an organic and relational approach to membership, service and leadership in a church context rich with small groups and ministry teams. People take on responsibility gradually—"tag along, try it on, take it on, pass it on" is our motto—with plenty of opportunity to "see how it goes" and "judge it by its fruit." This helps mitigate some of the disadvantages of not having formal disciplinary processes or qualification / application procedures.

In the case of homosexuality, this wasn't always the case. As I said, in the past, we did exclude people with same-sex partners. I don't mean that we discovered gay members and kicked them out of the church. If they were gay, they either didn't tell us or left before we could find out. But I did regularly tell potential new members that anyone in an active homosexual relationship should end this relationship (with pastoral help) before joining.

But this began to trouble me. It seemed to violate the Messianic call to "fair judgment" as seen in the Servant Song of Isaiah 11: 1-5. [85] I was troubled by my willingness to make accommodations for the acceptance of many remarried people (accommodations that I thought were pastorally justified) but unwilling to consider those same accommodations in the case of gay people.

I can only speculate about my reasons for this disparity. An openly gay person is, by definition, easy to identify. By comparison, I rarely asked about the marital history of those who were candidates for membership. I didn't inquire about a whole range of "lifestyle sins." These other sins defied clear definition.

I'm not asserting that this muddled approach is standard practice in other churches. I'm just saying it was my approach

---

85 Isaiah 11: 1-5. A shoot will spring from the stock of Jesse, a new shoot will grow up from his roots. On him will rest the spirit of Yahweh, the spirit of wisdom and insight, the spirit of counsel and power, the spirit of knowledge and fear of Yahweh: his inspiration will lie in fearing Yahweh. His judgment will not be by appearances. His verdict not given on hearsay. He will judge the weak with integrity and give a fair sentence for the humblest in the land. *New Jerusalem Bible.*

and it troubled me. The ugly fact is, I knew that on the "gay issue," a pastor is under intense scrutiny. If I allowed an openly gay member to join the church, I could expect push back. (We got it when we baptized our first openly gay person.) Other moral concerns don't provoke the same response. Knowing this affects pastors, makes them cautious, timid ... can I say, cowardly?

We know from experience that exclusion in its various forms (no membership, no communion, no serving in this or that capacity) is painful to the people excluded. Our church had become a refuge for those who suffered this treatment in other churches—unwed mothers who were stigmatized in their home congregations found their way to our church because we had an evening for Single Moms and their kids to enjoy a gourmet meal served by wait staff. This dinner was for them, a banquet feast in the kingdom of God.

There are several moral languages used in the Bible: harm and care, justice and fairness, freedom and liberty, authority, loyalty, sanctity-purity. [86] When enforcing an exclusion from participation in the church and her ministry, a pastor takes the question of harm into account. By "harm," I don't mean "hurting someone's feelings," but placing an obstacle in the path of their pursuit of Christ, the path of human flourishing. We have to consider harm to the community as well as the individual. But harm is an important consideration.

We have the biblical rule to consider: "Loves does no harm to the neighbor" (Romans 13: 10). Jesus and the apostles emphasized love of neighbor as the epitome, summary and guiding principle of the law and the prophets. Presumably, this rule was given precisely to prevent harming people for religious reasons.

---

86 I am grateful to Jonathan Haidt for identifying these. Haidt, Jonathan. *The Righteous Mind: Why Good People Are Divided by Politics and Religion.* New York, N.Y.: Pantheon Books, 2012.

Let's Apply the Bible's Ultimate Ethic: The Rule of Love

Whether the sexual dimension of monogamous gay relationships is sinful, the ultimate ethic of Scripture would lead us to make much greater space for gay, lesbian, and transgender members than is the current practice in most churches.

It's a rather obvious point, but one that has been obscured in American evangelical circles.

Consider just how weighty the rule of love is in the New Testament:

"Honor your father and your mother: and, you shall love your neighbor as yourself." (Matthew 19:19)

"Jesus said unto him, you shall love the Lord your God with all your heart, and with all your soul, and with all your mind. This is the first and great commandment. And the second is like it, you shall love your neighbor as yourself." (Matthew 22:37-39)

"And the second is like, namely this, you shall love your neighbor as yourself. There is none other commandment greater than these." (Mark 12:31)

"And he answering said, you shall love the Lord your God with all your heart, and with all your soul, and with all your strength, and with all your mind; and your neighbor as yourself." (Luke 10:27)

"Love worketh no ill to his neighbor: therefore love is the fulfilling of the law." (Romans 13:10)

"For all the law is fulfilled in one word, even in this; 'you shall love thy neighbor as thyself.'" (Galatians 5:14)

"If you fulfill the royal law according to the scripture, you shall love your neighbor as yourself, you do well." (James 2:8)

I must admit that my evangelical self harbored a suspicion when I heard the "love ethic" emphasized. Wasn't this ethic prominent in the Liberal Protestant reading of Scripture? I had to shake off my bias and take a deeper look at this. I was surprised to find how *prominent* this is in the New Testament: Jesus, Paul, and James (not to mention John, who uses different language for the same notion) all emphasize it. This was an important part of the apostolic tradition in the wake of Jesus. It seems to me that this ethic is emphasized so strongly precisely because the Jesus movement knew all too well the danger of over-zealous or harmful application of the Bible.

The words of an old hymn come to mind:

> *But we make His love too narrow*
> *By false limits of our own;*
> *And we magnify His strictness*
> *With a zeal He will not own.*
> *For the love of God is broader*
> *Than the measure of the mind;*
> *And the heart of the Eternal*
> *Is most wonderfully kind.*
>
> —**Frederick William Faber 1814-1863**

We are *supposed* to listen to the voice within us that says, "Gosh, this just doesn't sound loving, even though it sounds correct!" Of course, there's much sorting to be done: what does love really call for in a given situation? Nevertheless, the warning in Scripture is there for a reason.

For several years, I served as leader in The Word of God, a renewal-oriented community that had a monastic quality, even though it included many married people. We had high standards for admittance and participation, along with a more vigorous approach to discipline, including exclusion when those standards weren't met. There were advantages to this approach. The community became an epicenter of the charismatic renewal in the Roman Catholic Church and contributed to charismatic renewal in many other churches. At its zenith, it numbered three thousand people (adults and children). But there were also disadvantages and they had to do with exclusion, which operated formally and informally through an intense and well-focused community culture. I saw first-hand the harm that can result from an over-zealous exercise of exclusion. It's fair to say that I became sensitized, more cautious, and sober regarding the dangers involved in exclusion.

Those who support exclusionary policies (often over a pet issue) become more reluctant the closer they are to the process of actually implementing the exclusion. For example, in our church, one of the most difficult things for a small group or ministry team leader to do is to say to someone who is disrupting the group: "If this behavior doesn't change, I will have to ask you to leave the group or team." Group leaders sometimes let the group "die a natural death" rather than ask the offending party to leave the group if they can't participate in a way that doesn't harm the people in the group.

Enforcing exclusion is a responsibility of leadership and to neglect it can cause its own harm. As Regional Overseer for 115 Vineyard churches, I met with pastors who needed to be told to step down. I sometimes had to assure them or their boards that the denomination would insist. In my local church, I have personally confronted men or women involved in adulterous affairs. I've told them that they cannot continue to serve in a particular ministry, for example, if they don't repent. I have asked men who have left their wives for other women to stop attending the church, so their wife can continue to come without the pain of seeing them every week. It's not fun, but I have done this with a clear conscience.

Yet, in this case, I slowly came to the conviction that the practice of exclusion, including categorical disqualification from ministry for gay, lesbian or transgender people [87] was too harmful to continue. It didn't pass the love test. I had to quietly assent to my conscience: I couldn't continue to exclude gay, lesbian or transgender people in this way any longer.

---

87 The moral questions related to transgender issues are too different from homosexuality to treat in this letter. But I came to think that transgender people need our pastoral attention and help in making thoughtful moral discernments rather than simply excluding them categorically. Facing these issues after returning to Ann Arbor shaped my thinking profoundly.

Once I had squared with my changing conscience on this matter, I noticed that we began to see more gay people (women mostly) who were powerfully drawn to the church. By that I mean, they shared stories of being *led* here, of feeling a powerful connection when they arrived, of experiencing God in new and transforming ways. Most came in pre-existing exclusive partnerships, committed to monogamy. Some had children they cared for.

I remember one woman who had been raised in a cultish, quasi-Christian setting, sitting in my office, telling me her story. Of powerful same-sex attraction from childhood, of coming out to her family and being ostracized, of spiraling downward in her life, of reaching out to God, of finding him in our worship. She wanted to know if she could receive baptism to express her newfound commitment to Christ. Could she be part of the church family? I said yes. Her eyes filled with tears at the prospect. I couldn't help but think "Many people feel they are doing *us* a favor by selecting us as their church home after shopping around for a church that best suits their needs. When was the last time I saw someone so deeply moved just to be included—as though she was surprised by this good news? This woman is like one of the Gentiles of old, approaching a predominantly Jewish church in the new Jesus movement, showing the same, 'I can't believe this!' delight at simply being accepted."

When she asked me directly about her status as a woman in a same-sex relationship, I said something to this effect: "I've been wrestling with this question for some time now. When the Scripture addresses same-sex issues, the texts are uniformly negative. I've concluded that one of two things is the case. One, there is a reasonable case to be made that what the texts are addressing is something other than today's monogamous relationships between two people committed to each other for life. Another possibility is that the traditional reading is correct. Even then, we accept people who violate other biblical standards, like remarriage after divorce. We make accommodations because it seems like the right thing to do, all things considered. At the end of the day, these seem to me like debatable issues. We can agree to disagree. We are ultimately accountable to God for our actions. We can accept each other without approving each other's moral standing on this or that issue. God does, or we couldn't be saved. That's the gospel, isn't it?"

It was an important moment for me as a pastor. "Did I just say that?" I thought. "It makes sense. I can't argue with what I just said. Oh my, I've landed somewhere on this issue, haven't I?"

I am still in awe of the courage this young woman demonstrated by simply coming to our church and setting up the appointment to meet me that day. I marvel at the love for Jesus that must have moved her to seek to be in a community with other Christians without knowing for sure that she would be welcomed with open arms. Who does this?

More came with stories equally moving. I don't share them here because those who come our way sense that we are a church in transition on this issue and they don't have any interest in drawing attention to themselves. It takes more courage for them to attend our church than it takes for most people. But they are here, many having entered committed partnerships, some with children they are raising together. And I realize I am their pastor. It's my job to make a place for them here.

But with so much riding on this particular issue, I felt the need for a larger framework in which to place this one. With or without such a framework, I knew that I couldn't enforce the whole range of exclusionary policies [88] in good conscience. The ambiguity in the prohibitive texts, based on a careful reading that takes their historical context into account, combined with the self-evident harm—to gay people and the

---

88 By "exclusionary policies," I mean exclusion from baptism, membership, and categorical disqualifications from ministry positions, including leadership.

Christian mission—was enough for me. But in the face of such intense controversy, I also longed for a biblical approach that would allow the church to maintain unity in the Spirit, despite differing convictions on this question and others like it. When this controversy has run its course, another will be upon us. Must Christians who otherwise share so much in common, who *belong together*, inevitably split over such issues?

There is something unhelpful—"demonic" is another word that comes to mind—about the intensity of this controversy. Is this intensity simply a function of the vexing questions that this controversy raises? Of course: sex, marriage, faithfulness to God, respect for Scripture, are all huge concerns for people of faith. But does the intensity of the controversy—the anxiety, the anger, the readiness to break off relationship—create anything but a hostile environment *for everyone*? We see this playing out in society every day on the cable entertainment news shows. We see it playing out in the church. It's shameful. We're aping something that has nothing to do with the Kingdom of God, claiming moral superiority as we do. It is not enough to have different beliefs from a world gone mad, if in the process we adopt the same patterns of thinking that fuel the madness. [89]

Isn't there help in Scripture for just such a dilemma?

But I had a further desire—to find a framework that would help me understand the gospel itself more deeply. In the midst of our madness, God is also sovereign. He reigns. There must be some higher purpose in all the intense pressure thrust upon us by this controversy. There must be some redemptive purpose in all this—a blessing beyond all this anguish.

What do we not understand or appreciate about the gospel that could help us find our way out of this mess?

---

89 "And be not conformed to this world: but be transformed by the renewing of your mind, that you may prove what is that good, and acceptable, and perfect, will of God." (Romans 12:2)

Needed: A Way to Handle Controversial Issues

I'm proposing an approach that respects the differing convictions of those who disagree and emphasizes the gospel demand of acceptance (over affirmation on the one hand, and over exclusion on the other.) In fact, I think I had implicitly spoken from within such a framework when I answered the woman who came to ask me about baptism. In effect, I told her that the question of how God thought of her being lesbian was an example of what the Bible calls a "disputable matter." It was a category that I naively assumed to be widely accepted in the Christian tradition. I have since come to see that it is has been largely obscured by the tradition of the church. It is articulated in Romans 14-15, and thus deeply rooted in the gospel.

My rather idiosyncratic experience as a pastor set me up to appreciate the fact that the Spirit can draw people together in a powerful unity, despite very significant differences of belief and conviction.

My wife, Nancy, and I led communal households that included our growing family and up to eight single people at a time. We lived communally with sixty other adults (mostly single) over that period. We shared breakfast and dinner together most days, morning prayers, and Saturday chores. We took vacations together. For ten years, we practiced common finances in a network of several such households, including ones for men and women committed to a life of monastic celibacy. The church that eventually became the Vineyard Church of Ann Arbor started in our living room and became one of four "church fellowships" in a covenant relationship with each other (Roman Catholic, Presbyterian, Lutheran and our loosely evangelical congregation.) By measures used to mark devotion in my own denomination, this experience of Christian community far exceeded the commitment level in the most vibrant churches, including our own today. [90]

90 I would estimate, conservatively, that over 80 percent of the members tithed, and over 90 percent participated in small groups and

We enjoyed this level of mutual commitment despite serious dogmatic disagreements, having to do with the gospel itself (justification by faith, for example). We disagreed over practices with profound moral implications (whether devotion to Mary constituted idolatry, for example). Over a period of years, the community devolved into a form of authoritarianism and legalism. Nancy and I, like so many others, became renewal movement refugees. We found in the Vineyard's "mere Christianity" approach—unity by virtue of a shared experience of a common core—a return to what we felt was the most prophetic and powerful dimension of our ecumenical community experience.

That there is a powerful center—mediated by a risen Lord manifesting himself through the Spirit—a center that unites people from different backgrounds with different convictions on important matters that often divide others, is something I know from thirty years of experience in both movements. To deny it is to deny my experience of the Risen Lord.

But what is the biblical teaching that makes this possible? Oddly, mystifyingly, I've never heard it articulated. I now believe that Romans 14-15 is integral to such an articulation and I offer it in summary form now.

The nub of the matter is covered in Romans 14. [91]

---

some form of regular service, and most were in regular contact with a designated pastoral care leader.

91 Receive him that is weak in the faith, but not to doubtful disputations. For one believes that he may eat all things: another, who is weak, eats herbs. Let not him that eats despise him that does not eat; and let not him who eats not judge him that eats: for God has received him. Who are you that judges another man's servant? to his own master he stands or falls. Yet, he shall be held up: for God is able to make him stand. One man holds one day above another: another esteemeth every day alike. Let every man be fully persuaded in his own mind. He that regards the day, regards it unto the Lord; and he that regards not the day, to the Lord he does not regard it. He that eats, eats to the Lord, for he gives God thanks; and he that eats not, to the Lord

A growing chorus of scholars [92] agree that Romans has been misread by artificially dividing it into two largely separate sections: Paul's articulation of the gospel in the first eight chapters, followed by his treatment of miscellaneous concerns in the next eight chapters. Instead, there is a strong consensus that Romans 9-11, 12-13, and 14-15 are the main event as much as the first eight chapters.

Paul seems to be speaking to two groups within the Roman church, in danger of rending the unity of the Jesus community

---

he eats not, and gives God thanks. For none of us lives to himself, and no man dies to himself. For whether we live, we live unto the Lord; and whether we die, we die unto the Lord: whether we live therefore, or die, we are the Lord's. For to this end Christ both died, and rose, and revived, that he might be Lord both of the dead and living. But why do you judge your brother? or why do you look down on your brother? for we shall all stand before the judgment seat of Christ. For it is written, As I live, said the Lord, every knee shall bow to me, and every tongue shall confess to God. So then every one of us shall give account of himself to God. Let us not therefore judge one another any more: but judge this rather, that no man put a stumbling block or an occasion to fall in his brother's way. I know, and am persuaded by the Lord Jesus, that there is nothing unclean of itself: but to him that believes any thing to be unclean, to him it is unclean. But if your brother is grieved with your meat, you are now not walking charitably. Do not destroy him with your meat, for whom Christ died. Let not then your good be evil spoken of: For the kingdom of God is not meat and drink; but righteousness, and peace, and joy in the Holy Ghost. For he that in these things serves Christ is acceptable to God, and approved of men. Let us therefore follow after the things which make for peace, and things wherewith one may edify another. For meat destroy not the work of God. All things indeed are pure; but it is evil for that man who eats with offence. It is good neither to eat flesh, nor to drink wine, nor any thing whereby thy brother stumbles, or is offended, or is made weak. Have you faith? have it to yourself before God. Happy is he that

92 N.T. Wright, James Dunn, and Ben Witherington III are representative.

and thus damaging its powerful witness to the glorious gospel.
He characterizes these two groups with two terms: "the
weak" and "the strong." While not co-terminus with "Gentile
believers in Jesus" and "Jewish believers in Jesus," this more
basic category distinction is in the background.

At the time of the writing of Romans (54-58 A.D.) [93] Jewish
believers in Jesus are returning with their non-messianic
Jewish brethren to Rome, after being exiled by decree of
Claudius (roughly in the late 40s A.D.) In the meantime, the
predominantly messianic Jewish community has become a
predominantly Gentile Christian community. [94] There were big
and understandable tensions emerging as the Messianic Jews
seek to re-integrate with the come-lately Gentiles in a position
of newfound power.

For reasons debated in the literature, less is known with
certainty about these two groups—the weak and the strong—
than we would hope. The weak are marked by two concerns:
they are vegetarians abstaining from the eating of meat (and
some, wine too) and they observe "special days." The strong,
contra the weak, eat meat and do not observe "special days"
(or do so in a lax way). Dunn and others indicate that the lack
of precision in defining these groups more carefully may be
to allow for a broad application of concerns facing the Roman
church. [95]

Paul urges each group to welcome or accept the other
despite differences that threaten to tear them apart. Practically,
this means that they are to maintain or restore the table
fellowship that was the centerpiece of Christian fellowship in

93 Osborne, *Romans The IVP New Testament Commentary Series*, p. 13.
94 These dates seem not to be widely contested; see Wright, N. T. *The
New Interpreter's Bible : Acts - First Corinthians: Volume 10*. Nashville,
Tenn.: Abingdon Press, 2002. pp. 406-407 for a discussion of the
historical occasion of the letter.
95 Jewett, *Romans: A Commentary*, p. 388; Dunn, James. D. G. Word
Biblical Commentary: Volume 38A, Romans 1-8. Nashville, Tenn.:
Thomas Nelson, 1988, p. 801

the first 125 years of the church. [96] Their witness to the gospel seems to be at stake.

As N.T. Wright [97] and others have shown, the gospel according to Paul is articulated as a message subversive to the gospel of the Roman Emperor. "Jesus is Lord" infers, "and Caesar is not." In the context of Romans 14-15, Caesar's claim to lordship is demonstrated in his remarkable capacity to hold an ethnically, religiously and culturally diverse empire together by his strength (primarily military). Paul, it is

---

96 Taussig, Hal. *In the Beginning was the Meal.* Minneapolis, inn.N: Fortress Press, 2009.

97 In citing Wright, whose commentary on Romans I found quite helpful, I do not wish to imply that Wright does anything but vigorously deny that homosexuality is anything but immoral in every enacted expression. He does, however say that what his own communion has done is to have a shouting match over this issue rather than a reasoned debate. Which of course, begs the question: how can we engage in such a debate? My proposal is that we do so as friends in community with Christ and each other, helpfully informed by Paul's teaching in Romans 14-15. If, at the outset, we exclude Romans 14-15 from consideration, we will have chosen, I think, the path of multiplied schism such as we have seen over the years on many other issues. Initial considerations in any reasoned dispute among friends would include the respective roles of Scripture, tradition, reason, and I might add, experience. As a pastoral travelogue of discernment that employs the Ignatian method, I have relied more heavily on experience—reasoned reflection on experience, interacting with Scripture and tradition, than I think Wright would as an Anglican. See: Wright, N. T. *Communion and Koinonia: Pauline Reflections on Tolerance and Boundaries.* A paper given at the Future of Anglicanism Conference, Oxford, 2002 and [[http://www.youtube.com/watch?v=YpQHGPGejKs]]. For more on the dismissal of experience as it played out in early 20th century American thought and institutions—and the consequences of that dismissal—see *"Writing Assessment's 'Debilitating Inheritance': Behaviorism's Dismissal of Experience."* by Maja Wilson, Dissertation, 2013, University of New Hampshire.

thought, is passionate about the unity of the church because according to his gospel, Jesus demonstrates a more powerful lordship than Caesar in that he holds an equally diverse community together without resorting to force. [98] He does so, in fact, by the power of God demonstrated in human weakness. He does so by the power of the crucified messiah, received by the church and demonstrated in her life together, harbinger of the coming kingdom of God breaking into the present in surprising ways that are easy to miss unless one has eyes to see and ears to hear.

Even conservative scholars like James Dunn see the weak as corresponding to modern day conservatives and the strong corresponding to modern day liberals. [99] That is, in a loose shorthand, those who feel more bound to the strictures of law and those who feel free from these strictures. It fits: Paul warns the weak (conservatives) to stop judging the strong and he warns the strong (liberals) to stop treating the weak dismissively, with contempt. [100]

So the critical question is: what were the actual issues dividing the weak from the strong in the Roman church?

If the answer to that question is "matters of relative insignificance or indifference," the category is, in a sense, less robust or even moot. By that I mean it is unable to help the church maintain a unity in the Spirit that is stronger than the tensions placed on the community when divergent views emerge on this question and others like it. Without Romans 14-15 or something like it, such differences, it seems, *must* divide us. The heritage of church splits that followed in the wake of the Protestant Reformation is inevitable. As the

---

98 *New Interpreters Bible: Romans*, by N.T. Wright, p. 739, 750

99 Dunn, *Word Biblical Commentary*, p. 803

100 One can't help but note that today's conservatives seem to produce angry commentators, pointing the finger at liberals, while liberals produce comedians who make a living from contemptuous humor aimed at conservatives.

surrounding society becomes more diverse, we should expect, even welcome, more of the same.

If Romans 14-15 applies to very hotly contested differences today, church-rending differences not easily resolved by appeal to the normal means, it would be a more robust category. That is, it would actually help us to maintain a unity in the Spirit in the face of big differences. The church would have a powerful tool to help her witness in a world flying apart.

In my search of the literature, I discovered a range of possibilities, a more robust and less robust kind of "weak" vs. "strong," depending on the particular issues thought to be included in the categories. [101] If, for example, the vegetarians avoided meat or special days for merely ceremonial reasons, then the category is not so helpful for the kinds of controversies threatening the unity of the church today. But many commentators suggest that the weak and the strong were divided over very serious moral concerns. James Dunn has this to say: "The issue then which confronts Paul here is not a slight or casual one. Those today who think he was making too much fuss over some peculiarities of diet (simply a matter of a few vegetarians), or particular feast days (one or two more holy days), have completely missed the point. The issue was far more serious than that." [102]

The vegetarianism of the weak, for example, may have been prompted by concerns about idolatry. Eating meat sacrificed to idols (the explicit concern of 1 Corinthians 8-10) could have been understandably regarded as participation in idolatry. [103] The butcher shops in Rome at the time were

---

101 The most careful and exhaustive scholarship on this question that I could find was from Reasoner, Mark. *The Strong and the Weak: Romans 14:1–15:13 in Context*, Cambridge, UK: Cambridge University Press, 1999. See his carefully argued conclusions, pp. 218-219.

102 Dunn *Word Biblical Commentary*, p. 811.

103 Several commentaries include this as a reasonable candidate for the vegetarianism of the weak, including *Romans* by N.T. Wright; *Word Biblical Commentary* by Dunn; D. Martyn-Lloyd Jones. *Romans:*

connected to pagan temples. The sacrificial animal would be slaughtered as an offering to the gods. The power of the deity would be invoked over those who ate the meat. One can see how Jewish believers and conscientious Gentiles influenced by Moses would be careful to avoid eating meat so as not to have concourse, potentially, with demons or to act in violation of the first commandment. [104]

The vegetarianism of the weak may have been to avoid meat improperly drained of blood. [105] While this practice is widely considered acceptable to many Christians today, there is strong biblical reason to avoid it, even for those not obligated to keep kosher. After all, this practice was first introduced in the book of Genesis in the time of Noah, to reinforce the sanctity of life—the image of God in humanity.

The Noahide Code—a set of imperatives in Genesis 9:4-6 [106] given for the "children of Noah," i.e. all humankind after the flood—was tied to the idea that "the life is in the blood." This was a matter of special concern because "in the image of God

---

Exposition of Chapter 14:1-17, Liberty and Conscience. East Peoria, Ill.: Versa Press, 2011; *The Strong and the Weak* by Reasoner, p. 218.

104 Douglas Moo notes that "Jews would sometimes abstain from wine, something Paul mentions in Romans 14, out of concern that it had been tainted by offering the wine as a libation to the gods." Moo, Douglas J. *The Epistle to the Romans, The New International Commentary on the New Testament,*. Grand Rapids, Mich.: Eerdmans, 1996. p. 831.

105 Commentators who include this include Stott, John. *The Message of Romans: God's Good News for the World*. p. 356; Wright, *Romans* p. 735; Dunn, *Word Biblical Commentary*, p. 801; Jewett, *Romans: A Commentary*, p. 838; Reasoner, *The Strong and the Weak*, p. 218.

106 " But flesh with the life thereof, which is the blood thereof, you shall not eat. And surely your blood of your lives will I require; at the hand of every beast will I require it, and at the hand of man; at the hand of every man's brother will I require the life of man. Whoever sheds man's blood, by man shall his blood be shed: for in the image of God made he man."

has God made humankind." Some Christians in Africa and elsewhere abide by these rulings today.

Indeed some think the Noahide Code may have been in the background of the Jerusalem council's ruling that Gentiles should avoid meat sacrificed to idols and meat improperly drained of blood. [107] One can imagine that as the Jewish community left Rome in the late 40's A.D., the kosher butchers left with them and the Gentile believers became accustomed to eating such meat without scruples. Read anachronistically, this is not a first order moral issue today, but read in its original context, it may well have been.

Dunn takes this view: "What seems to be in view is the condemnation by 'the weak' of the conduct of 'the strong'; that is the firmly held judgment that the conduct is unacceptable, which in this context means 'unacceptable to God.' The one who does not eat evidently regards *not* eating as of crucial importance in maintaining the relationship with God, so that *eating* becomes an act unacceptable to God, an act, that is to say, which merits divine condemnation." [108]

N.T. Wright echoes Dunn here: "One may imagine that for some of the 'weaker' Christians in Rome the idea of eating meat that had not been certified as kosher, or that had been offered to idols, would seem just as 'pagan' and hence evil as sexual immorality; indeed, granted the connection between idol-worship and licentious orgies, one can understand their point of view." [109]

Similarly, with the concern of the weak over "special days." If the matter in Rome had to do say, with the observance of Roman special days, a possibility mentioned in the literature, then we have a low or non-controversial issue. This is even more so in our time, unless we consider the use of the modern

---

107 Acts 15:29 That you abstain from meats offered to idols, and from blood, and from things strangled, and from fornication: from which if you keep yourselves, you shall do well. Farewell.

108 Dunn, *Word Biblical Commentary*, p. 802, italics in the original.

109 N. T. Wright, *Romans,* p. 750.

terms for the days of the week to be a participation in the idols they are named after. But highly regarded commentators see more significant issues than this behind the controversy.

Stott, Dunn and others regard Sabbath-keeping as a likely candidate of the concern over "special days." [110] D. Marty Lloyd-Jones and other older commentators insist that Sabbath-keeping is ruled out precisely because it is a matter of the moral, not the ceremonial law. [111] But this seems to only beg the question and exemplifies the tendency to interpret the category in light of what we already consider to be legitimately disputable or not.

Take Sabbath-keeping, a matter that has receded to the status of a secondary moral or even a "merely ceremonial" concern in the contemporary church. Indeed, there is a strong case to be made that observance of the Sabbath is binding on Christians. It is, after all, a command enshrined in the Ten Commandments. Even more, it is embedded in creation— God having rested from his work on the seventh day. In this sense, Sabbath-breaking could be regarded as a sin against nature, because it violates God's created order.

So what do we have in Romans 14-15: a robust category that can help us maintain unity in the face of serious moral and doctrinal differences, or one that simply helps us when dealing matters of relative indifference? I think the preponderance of evidence, not least the sheer length and vigor of Paul's treatment (two chapters in his magisterial letter), suggest that Paul includes first order moral concerns in his disputable issues category. That is, he is using this category to deal with concerns that threatened the unity of

---

110 Stott, John. *The Message of Romans*, p. 356; Dunn, *Word Biblical Commentary*, p. 805; Jewett, *Romans: A Commentary*, p. 844; Wright, *Romans*, p. 736; Fitzmyer, Joseph A,. *Romans: The Anchor Yale Bible Commentaries*. New Haven, Conn.T: Yale University Press, 1993. p. 690; Reasoner, *The Strong and the Weak*, p. 219; Moo, *The Epistle to the Romans*, p. 842

111 *Romans, Liberty and Conscience*, D. Martyn Lloyd-Jones, p. 81.

the church in Rome, and for good reason. These included the kind of concerns that were hotly contested group boundary marker issues in their time and required all of Paul's powers to persuade the Roman believers to see them as "disputable," as matters over which *not* to divide for the sake of the gospel. [112]

The Lord knows we live in a highly polarized time when a robust category like this would be needed to maintain unity in the face of great diversity. Our readiness to break fellowship over lesser matters is indication of the need. We mourn this divisive spirit until it comes to a controversy over which we feel great passion, then we can hardly believe good Christians could differ in good conscience over such a thing.

Treat This as a Disputable Matter

This category has helped me to see the promise in a third way approach to the gay issue—one that moves beyond the binary set up by the "open and affirming" or "love the sinner, hate the sin" code phrases. I think it is reasonable to regard this limited question—how the biblical prohibitions apply to monogamous gay relationships—as a "disputable matter." By that, I do not mean that it is not controversial. In fact, controversy is a key component of disputable matters as Paul uses the term. Nor do I mean that it is not a matter of conscience. That too, is a mark of disputable matters. And I

---

112 In his paper *Communion and Koinonia: Pauline Reflections on Tolerance and Boundaries* Wright argues that the category only applies to questions like Sabbath or eating meat sacrificed to idols because these issues constitute "cultural boundary markers" for Israel, markers which could not apply to Gentile believers. But if Romans 14-15 is not helpful in moral disputes over matters as serious as the degree to which a person participates in the Emperor cult or the binding nature of one of the Ten Commandments (rooted in nature itself) then it seems useless in the case of any moral dispute that we might face. That may be, but if it is, we are left with ever-increasing division as our only alternative, especially in light of the challenging moral questions that will face the church in the coming century.

am definitely not applying this category to the homosexual acts that were so prominent in the biblical period— homosexual services demanded of slaves, homosexual relationships spawned in pederasty, and homosexual acts in the context of temple prostitution. I am only invoking this category to the question of how the Bible speaks to people in monogamous gay relationships seeking to maintain lifelong fidelity.

Before applying the perspective of Romans 14-15 as a third-way approach, let me summarize what I think are reasonable criteria for determining whether or not this category can inform the way we relate to each other over a controversial issue.

That there are disputable matters is commonly acknowledged. Yet, there is ongoing debate over which issues are regarded as belonging to the category. As N.T. Wright points out, Paul's categorization of the divisive issues in Rome as "disputable matters" would have been itself controversial. [113] This is an essential point to grasp. Paul is not dealing with matters that everyone regarded as "matters of moral indifference." [114] No. They warranted this treatment in this letter precisely because they were threatening the unity of the church in Rome. The same is true today. Yet every issue is not a disputable matter. This is implied by Paul's introduction of the category. What are reasonable criteria for inclusion in the category, "disputable matters"?

Paul doesn't offer explicit criteria from which we can generalize. But some can be reasonably inferred from the examples of weak and strong that he uses in the text, especially assuming a more robust reading. As background, I found Roger Olsen's book, *Mosaic of Christian Belief: Twenty*

---

113 See Wright, *New Interpreters Bible, The Letter to the Romans*, p. 738
114 Confusingly this term, *adiaphora*, which was borrowed by Tertullian and Chrysostom from stoic philosophy in which it referred precisely to questions without any moral significance, has often been conflated with Paul's "disputable matters" category.

Centuries of Unity in Diversity to be quite helpful in thinking through this question of criteria. Olsen distinguishes between three orders or levels of Christian truth.

Dogma: Olsen defines dogma as truths essential to Christianity itself; to deny them is to follow something other than Jesus. Christian identity is at stake. [115]

Dogma is another word for the foundation Paul laid in Corinth to keep Jews and Gentiles with all their differences together: Jesus Christ, his living, dying, rising, ascending, coming again.

According to the grace of God which is given to me, as a wise masterbuilder, I have laid the foundation, and another builds on it. But let every man take heed how he builds thereupon. For other foundation can no man lay than that is laid, which is Jesus Christ. Now if any man build upon this foundation gold, silver, precious stones, wood, hay, stubble; Every man's work shall be made manifest: for the day shall declare it, because it shall be revealed by fire; and the fire shall try every man's work of what sort it is. If any man's work abide which he has built thereupon, he shall receive a reward. If any man's work shall be burned, he shall suffer loss: but he himself shall be saved; yet so as by fire. (1 Corinthians 3:10-15)

In our church, dogma is defined not simply as "Jesus" but the Jesus of the canonical gospels and the historic creeds: the Apostles' and Nicene Creeds.

Doctrine: Olsen defines doctrine as a secondary category of teachings central to a particular tradition of Christians. These can be very significant matters that define entire traditions: predestination or free will; how we understand the saving work of Jesus; the nature of church and sacraments. It can be argued that many denominations were formed by raising such matters to the highest level of truth, a

---

115 Olsen, Roger E. *The Mosaic of Christian Belief: Twenty Centuries of Unity and Diversity.* Downer's Grove, IL: Inter Varsity Press, 2002. pp 44-45.

dynamic that has perhaps served unwittingly to diminish the significance of the disputable-matters category.

Opinion: Olsen defines opinion here as matters of speculative nature about which there is no consensus in the church (used in its broad sense.) Examples might include the age of earth, mode of baptism and criteria for ordination.

Echoing Wright (or perhaps Wright echoes Olsen) Olsen notes the obvious: that "there is no consensus among Christians" about which beliefs belong in which category. One person's opinion is another's doctrine, is another's dogma.

But with Olsen's distinctions in view, we can infer reasonable criteria based on Paul's "disputable matters."

1. When it doesn't involve a matter of basic Christian dogma such as we find in the great ecumenical creeds (Apostles, Nicene, Chalcedonian, etc.)

When dealing with matters central to the gospel itself, Paul can be ferocious and not in the least bit irenic, as virtually all of the Pauline letters attest. None of Paul's writings indicate that he considered these as disputable matters over which a diversity of perspectives could be tolerated without changing the nature of Christianity itself.

2. When the debate brings two or more biblical truths into dynamic tension (e.g. mercy-judgment, law-grace, free will-predestination) so that both parties make reasonable appeals to Scripture.

The Christian community doesn't depend on uniformity of perspective in all things for its unity. Like the people of Israel, it is bound together by shared set of *concerns* as well—to know God, his purposes, to follow his will, and so on. And it has a shared book, the Bible. If we're drawn together by a text, the text is the Bible. If we're arguing over the meaning of a text, the text is the Bible. Because we are a people of the Book. This limits and distinguishes the nature of our debates.

It doesn't take a great deal of imagination to see how controversies over eating meat sacrificed to idols, eating meat improperly drained of blood, or Sabbath observance, might have been hotly contested, with both sides making appeals to Scripture. In fact, if we discipline ourselves so as not to read the text anachronistically, we can imagine that "the weak" could muster very compelling arguments for their position using Scripture. These would have been presented as first order moral concerns by "the weak." Yet Paul, if anything, shows personal sympathy with the positions of "the strong."

3. *When faithful Christians take different views on the issue.*

The Spirit, and not just the devil, is at work in the church when disturbances over truth arise. Responding to the contemporary controversy by simply asserting that there is no legitimate debate to be had is an inadequate response. If we look back at many controversies of the past that have now been settled, we can appreciate this. Church history reveals that previous generations, often our betters in Christ, had significant blind spots. We might have them too. We can correct for this lack of humility by carefully engaging issues during the period when a previous consensus seems to be challenged by contrary views, especially when those raising the concerns are otherwise highly regarded.

As stated earlier with citation from Wright, the issues Paul placed in this category would have been vigorously contested as belonging to the category. Perhaps we shouldn't be surprised to find ourselves in a similar pickle. Whether or not this is so requires careful reading of the text, wading through a careful examination of what those issues might have been. It also requires a humble reading that calls us to let go of any time-bound bias. We don't read a text about how to handle controversial matters without our own hotly contested controversies crouching at the door, and this affects our reading. We have to be careful not to let this unduly affect us, especially if it means dismissing the relevance of Romans 14-15 without due care.

The casual reader of the Bible often neglects this. Good heavens, it strains my capacity and I'm paid to do it. But it is the sort of work pastors must do when charged with the solemn obligation of caring for the sheep of His pasture.

It's understandable that I would stress this, given my concerns with the traditional view. Minorities always have more to gain by tolerance of diversity. It would be natural for me to overstate how many share my concerns. Time will tell. I do know that people often share their concerns with those who might give them a sympathetic hearing. So it's not a surprise that I know many pastors who have "confided" similar concerns when they learn of mine. This confirms my sense that many are looking for a new way forward.

Of course, it is possible that the Bible prohibits all same-sex relationships that include sexual intimacy. Many take this view. In fact, it is so commonly assumed that many commentaries simply assert it without arguing carefully for it. But I am a pastor. When I am expected (or urged) to exclude those who otherwise bear the marks of the Spirit in their lives on the basis of these texts, I have to face the problems associated with applying the prohibitions to people in modern day monogamous gay relationships. While such relationships may be included in the prohibition, I can't simply dismiss the *credible* and *serious* objections to this assumption. Scripture may be silent on this question as it is on many issues of equal or greater significance. If it is speaking, it is not speaking clearly to this question—not nearly as clearly as it is speaking to male shrine prostitution, pederasty and sexual services demanded of slaves.

Even when matters of interpretation are resolved, application is another task. As Richard Hays points out, the New Testament statements on homosexuality are not formulated as rules. [116] Many, including those who hold a traditional view, would acknowledge that monogamous gay couples seeking to be faithful to each other and to Christ are not the primary aim of the prohibitions.

---

116 See his discussion of this in *Moral Vision of the New Testament*, p. 394-395.

So perhaps it's not surprising that Richard Hays, noted for his careful work in the field of New Testament ethics, refers to the church's response to modern day homosexuality as a debatable issue (without linking this explicitly to Paul's category in Romans 14-15) in *A Moral Vision of the New Testament*. Hays says, "This means that for the foreseeable future we must find ways to live within the church in a situation of serious moral disagreement while still respecting one another as brother and sisters in Christ. If the church is going to start practicing the discipline of exclusion from the community, there are other issues far more important than homosexuality where we should begin to draw a line in the dirt: violence and materialism, for example." [117]

I am convinced that how the biblical prohibitions apply to monogamous gay relationships is indeed a disputable matter and that the teaching of Romans 14-15 should guide our response.

---

117 Hays, *Moral Vision*, p. 400.

CHAPTER 5

The Gospel Way

Welcome and Wanted

APPLYING THE TEACHING of Romans 14-15 requires a deep understanding of the gospel. Following this teaching upholds and reveals the gospel's power. Walking in this path requires the full devotion of a disciple willing to die to self in order to follow the Risen Lord.

This provides the makings of a third way to guide pastors and local churches in the care of people in the face of the gay controversy. Our church, the Vineyard Church of Ann Arbor, is attempting to flesh this out. After lengthy consultation within our pastoral team and church board, we spoke one-on-one with our larger circle of leaders (about 70 small group and ministry team leaders) and I shared an earlier version of this letter with our leaders.

The term "third way" places this approach in the context of the two existing alternatives: "open and affirming" and "love the sinner, hate the sin." These two approaches are variously described, but they are marked by particular practices. These practices (inclusion on the one hand, exclusion on the other) are based on a definitive and shared (within their respective communities) view of the morality of monogamous gay relationships. Each alternative is based on treating the question as settled. The traditional view further insists that since all gay relationships are indisputably prohibited, exclusionary practices are justified. These practices include categorical disqualifications from ministry, especially leadership positions. [118]

In other words, to adopt either of the alternatives ("open and affirming" or "love the sinner, hate the sin") a church decides to *insist* on a common answer, judgment, or ruling on the question, denies that dispute is legitimate over this issue, and then works out a response from there. This approach is based on a shared assumption that this common ruling and its enforcement in the local congregation is necessary for the church to maintain "unity in the Spirit." The fundamental difference in the third way is that it does not share this assumption. A true unity of the Spirit is possible without adopting a common perspective on this question.

A third way departs from the "open and affirming" and the "love the sinner, hate the sin" approach by regarding the question of whether and how the biblical prohibitions apply in the case of monogamous gay relationships as a "disputable matter" in the Romans 14-15 sense.

In the heat of controversy, it helps to define the disagreement. In this letter, I have defined it in narrow, not broad terms. When engaging in a dispute with others, love

118 If the disqualification of women from leadership positions is any guide, then churches will draw the line in different places: some will disqualify those in gay relationships for service in children's ministry, small group leadership and the like; others will reserve disqualification for ordained ministry; eventually the disqualification will apply only to the most senior position of leadership. The purpose of the disqualification, wherever the line is drawn, is to signal to the congregation that the issue is settled: that monogamous gay relationships are clearly and definitively prohibitive because they are immoral.

and justice demands that we not exaggerate the disagreement. If we lived either in the time in which Leviticus was written or the Greco-Roman period of the Pauline epistles, we would be *surrounded* by a different homosexual ethic and practice, a different "homosexual lifestyle" than the one disputed in the church today. We would stand together as believers in condemning such practices. We would be on the same side.

But since that period, the question has narrowed. Are all monogamous gay couples, including the men and women we know who experience strong same-sex attraction, who may have struggled in vain against it as they became aware of it, who aspire to monogamous and faithful partnerships included in the biblical condemnations? Some might answer, clearly yes. Others might answer, clearly no. Still others might say, "It is not so clear."

A third approach says, "We can agree to disagree on this question" without separating from each other. We can hold our respective positions as firmly as our conscience dictates. But we have chosen not to treat this matter as something we have to hold in common in order to share a true unity of the Spirit.

Acceptance is the key biblical demand of a third way.

Jesus came to make a new way of belonging to God available to the Gentiles and in so doing, he shed new light on what it meant that Israel belongs to God as well. The key to this new way of belonging is the acceptance that is ours by virtue of the faithfulness of Jesus Christ, the centerpiece of the gospel. This powerful acceptance is expressed in very concrete ways when it comes to the differences we have over homosexuality.

A third way asks people who differ on this question to accept each other as Christ has accepted them, without predicating acceptance on affirming the other's lifestyle in this and many other moral questions.

In our church, we practice this on many other matters, including whether a particular remarriage constitutes ongoing adultery, whether a particular degree of consumption constitutes greed, whether using IVF to treat infertility is to participate in murder, and so on. Depending on how strong our convictions are on the question, such acceptance can be very demanding. It requires the power of the gospel to practice. We gladly embrace such demands because in so doing, we believe we are able to reveal, enact, and bear more powerful witness to the gospel.

A third way practices acceptance by choosing to respect the conscience of those who hold differing views, so long as they do so, "unto the Lord."

The demands of acceptance require us to maintain a relationship of honor and respect with those with whom we may ardently disagree. We accept the fact that our convictions on this matter differ, and those with whom we differ hold their convictions, as we do, unto the Lord. Inasmuch as this is not easy for us to do, we commit ourselves to bearing it as part of the disciple's cross. We don't agree to disagree by diminishing the importance of the question or by insisting that people care less about the issue. With Paul, we recognize that human beings, made in God's image, must strive toward integrity and unity. Violating one's conscience, even when it is mistaken, can do harm to that integrity. No one should urge anyone to do such a thing. We are not simply committed to helping others "do the right thing." We must also respect "the measure of faith" a person has received without attempting to persuade them to act against it, even if we would deem such actions to be right. We practice this form of acceptance by recognizing that each of us stands or falls, lives or dies, unto the Lord, trusting that the Lord is able to make even us wretched sinners stand. We ruthlessly practice the discipline of seeing those with whom we disagree in the best possible light, trusting God to judge their motives, intentions and heart better than we.

A third way urges disputants to recognize the limits of their personal responsibility for the actions of others and to leave the execution of a judgment to God.

There are very real questions about the meaning of the Jesus-Apostolic tradition summed up in "Don't judge!" in light of the need to make moral discriminations. But especially in the case of disputable matters, we are commanded to let God be the judge. In particular, we agree not to execute the judgment of separation from those with whom we disagree. We learn the lesson of the parable of the wheat and the tares, which urges the servants to weed less, knowing that the master does not trust them to weed well, leaving the final separation to his judgment on the last day. [119]

A third way provides time and space for a community to eventually resolve some disputes peacefully.

---

119 Matthew 13:24-30 Another parable put he forth to them, saying, The kingdom of heaven is likened to a man who sowed good seed in his field: But while men slept, his enemy came and sowed tares among the wheat, and went his way. But when the blade was sprung up, and brought forth fruit, then appeared the tares also. So the servants of the householder came and said unto him, Sir, did you not sow good seed in thy field? From whence then came the tares? He said to them, an enemy has done this. The servants said unto him, Would you like us to go and gather them up? But he said, No; in case while you gather up the tares, you root up also the wheat with them. Let both grow together until the harvest: and in the time of harvest I will say to the reapers, Gather together first the tares, and bind them in bundles to burn them: but gather the wheat into my barn.

Allowing the tension of a disputable matter provides time for the practical evidence, for the fruit of the two positions to become manifest. Time, a power over which we have no control, is allowed to function as a judge as well. This is the wisdom of Gamaliel, recorded in Acts. [120] Disputable matters may remain in dispute indefinitely, or with time, a common discernment may form in the community, and the dispute disappears, as is the case historically with other issues (Sabbath observance, women in leadership, slavery, etc.) The third way provides room for the Spirit to work in the community—to practice acceptance during the period of disagreement and to eventually settle some matters.

Churches following a third way practice thoroughgoing acceptance—embrace, not exclusion.

The appeal to mutual acceptance in Romans 14-15 requires a non-exclusionary approach. Those among "the weak" might well have wanted to impose various kinds of separation, exclusion, or leadership limitations on those who didn't share their convictions. Their views would have been buttressed by appeal to Scripture. The same could be said for the "the strong" who were in a position of sociological strength with respect to the returning Jewish contingent. [121] However, both groups are called to practice embrace, not exclusion or separation. Therefore, Christians in gay or lesbian partnerships committed to fidelity, are accepted for the sake of Christ. They are embraced, not excluded from full participation in the life of the community. Christians who believe such relationships

120 Acts 5: 38-39 And now I say unto you, Refrain from these men, and let them alone: for if this counsel or this work is of men, it will come to naught: But if it be of God, you cannot overthrow it; lest you be found to fight against God.

121 In conservative evangelical churches, those with "strong" convictions are in the minority, a significant difference in today's situation regarding the gay controversy.

to be sinful are accepted for the sake of Christ. They are embraced, not excluded, from full participation in the life of the community. In a word, they are wanted as full members of the community.

When asked if I will practice exclusion or commit myself to disqualifying a person in a gay relationship from ministry (usually some leadership position) I must decline to do so as a matter of conscience. I realize that this causes some distress for those who are convinced that it is necessary. But I believe the gospel, in this case, forbids me from doing so. Romans 14 is urging the church to err, in these matters, on the side of inclusion, to practice acceptance—embrace, not exclusion.

Let me expand on my reasons for not "splitting the difference" by accepting people who are gay as members but categorically disqualifying them from certain leadership positions. When we single this issue out as the basis for a categorical disqualification from ministry we are practicing a form of indirect or *de facto* exclusion. We are saying to an entire group of people in the church and beyond: you cannot be trusted to do (fill in the blank). You cannot be full participants in this church, even if in every other respect your service here is exemplary. Such disqualification from ministry is not consistent with how we handle the legitimate disputes over equivalent moral concerns.

Furthermore, a categorical exclusion from ministry, including from leadership, is not consistent with our overall approach to leadership. We take an inclusive and empowering approach to leadership, believing that all Christians are called to the work of ministry. In a church like ours, the lines between "ministry" and "leadership" are not sharply drawn. We cast a wide, not a narrow net for leadership in our church. In fact, what many churches call leadership we view as simple discipleship: people grow as they step into responsibility to care for others and make the church work.

The sharp distinction between "clergy" and "laity," common to other settings, does not exist in ours, in keeping with our forward leaning kingdom emphasis. The call to discipleship is a call to influence. All are called to be "fishers of people." Our task in empowering leaders is to ask, "Who is doing this already?"

Richard Hays supports a traditional reading on homosexuality, and comes from a tradition that supports the clergy-laity distinction. Remarkably, Hays says this: "The ensuing struggle (over gay ordination) has had the unfortunate effect of reinforcing a double standard for clergy and lay morality; it would be far better to articulate a single set of moral norms that apply to all Jesus' followers. Strictures against homosexuality belong in the church's moral catechesis, not in its ordination requirements. It is arbitrary to single out homosexuality as a special sin that precludes ordination. (Certainly, the New Testament does not do this.) The church has no analogous special rules to exclude from ordination the greedy or the self-righteous. Such matters are left to the discernment of the bodies charged with examining candidates for ordination; these bodies must determine whether the individual candidate has the gifts and graces requisite for ministry." [122]

Consistent with our ministry, in the culture of the Vineyard Church of Ann Arbor (substantially different from the culture of, say, the United Methodist Church) we rely heavily on holistic discernments about who is called and capable to lead in different ways. We don't receive applicants who have graduated from training centers in other cities, and send them through a job interview process. We get to know people as members of our local congregation—the congregation they would serve as future leaders—and observe their effectiveness, testing the fruit of their service as they take on more responsibility. We ask questions like "Do people respect them? Do people respond to their influence? Do they have the gifts to be effective? Are they kind? Do they harm the community

---

122 Hays, *Moral Vision.* p. 403

through gossip and slander? Can they keep a confidence? Are they reliable? Are they good to their word?"

To suspend this holistic approach in the case of a gay person and say, "You are not to be considered for these roles of service because you are gay regardless of any other factors in your life," would be punitive in effect. This would, furthermore, constitute a definitive and common ruling on the gay person's moral status, the very thing we refrain from doing because we treat this as a disputable matter. [123] This is especially problematic when we don't make categorical disqualifications for other disputable matters.

But there is another reason not to adopt such an approach. To do so will hurt the mission of the church among the modern day Gentiles. In our setting, these are left-leaning, science-friendly, religiously-averse Ann Arborites.

To cite one example: We received an e-mail inquiry recently from a lesbian couple looking for a church. It said, "We tried some open and affirming churches, but—and we don't mean to sound judgmental—there wasn't enough Jesus there. Would you accept us in your church?" We said, in a word, "Yes." I believe that we are called to be a church that reaches these modern day Gentiles.

We can infer that the position of "the strong" in Rome had an invigorating effect on the mission of the church. Paul did not abandon his Jewish identity. We can't assume that he renounced *torah* observance as appropriate for Jewish believers. Why would he side with "the strong" unless their approach advanced the mission among the Gentiles?

More Gentiles in Rome gained greater access to the church and her gospel because the strong didn't sort people on the basis of their eating meat sacrificed to idols or improperly

---

123 This is not to say that church members, including leaders, might not hold personal opinions about their moral status. But those who do so agree not to insist on imposing separation, exclusion, or ministry-leadership limitations on people who are gay or lesbian, just as we do not do this for other equivalent moral concerns.

drained of blood, despite the weighty arguments against these practices. They didn't sort people based on Sabbath day observance despite the weighty case that could be mustered to support such observance. The effect was to open the doors to the Gentiles. Their ensuing discipleship to Jesus would focus on other matters than these.

This gave time for the "strong" to demonstrate whether these Gentiles could become faithful followers of Jesus or not. The same is true today. The "strong" in Ann Arbor say that gay people in committed relationships are no worse morally than traditional married couples. The "weak" say the Bible argues against this. A third way allows this disagreement to play out until the "strong" can be shown to be right or wrong. If the "weak" are right, the absence of fruit will be self-evident. In the meantime, the gospel can reach the "strong" in Ann Arbor.

A third way challenges "conservatives" and "liberals" on this issue in different ways.

Using the parallel of so many commentators who see "the weak" as corresponding to "conservatives" (those with stricter scruples) and the "strong" as "liberals" (those without such scruples) we can apply the wisdom of Romans 14-15. I use these contemporary terms with much trepidation. They are loaded with so much freight. But so are the terms that Paul used, "weak" and "strong." At any rate, I beg the reader's indulgence. In a nod to the difficulties and inconsistencies inherent in such terms, I'll suffer the awkwardness of placing them in quotes at the beginning of each paragraph to remind us that some who have moral objections to homosexuality of all kinds would not identify with the current use of the term, "conservative." Similarly, some who do not have moral objections to homosexuality of all kinds would not take on the label, "liberal."

The "conservative" is challenged to accept those who don't share his moral objections. Conservatives are challenged not to separate from those who are "liberal" on this basis, but to embrace them instead. They accept the person in a monogamous gay partnership as a person for whom Christ died and more to the point, as a full member of Christ's body with them. Some conservatives will treat the person's homosexuality as "dross," something that will be "burned up" when the day comes, while the practicing gay brother or lesbian sister will be saved. Others may wonder if the brother or sister will indeed be saved in the last day if they haven't repented. They must trust the Spirit, who is ultimately responsible, to reveal what is needed for salvation to each person. They must accept the fact that it is not their job, in this case, to pressure their brother or sister to agree with them.

A third way is an opportunity for conservative families to teach their children how to be faithful to Jesus in a pluralistic age.

Depending on the convictions of the "conservative," this requires enormous restraint, a radical relinquishment of the desire to condemn or separate or to withhold acceptance. It is not an easy path to follow. This becomes especially challenging as the conservative raises children in a church pursuing a third way on this issue. The challenges faced by conservatives are equivalent to the challenges faced by the weak in the Roman church. Imagine raising children to observe the Sabbath as a moral obligation in a church that had mixed perspectives on this. Or in the more challenging case: imagine raising children to renounce eating meat sacrificed to idols in a church in which families had other perspectives on the issue.

The third way challenges "conservative" parents to help their children practice one of the key skills of discipleship: the ability to live out convictions that are not shared by others. Some will view this as an opportunity. Others will view it simply as a cross to bear for the sake of the gospel. I believe it is an opportunity for discipleship. In a third way approach, children can learn to practice within the church community skills that will come in handy outside the church community, where diversity of thought and practice will be even greater.

We live in a pluralistic age. Our children will need to learn how to hold their convictions despite the fact that others, including people they love and admire, do not share them. Sometimes parents of young children overestimate the effect of shielding their children from such differences. Even when we send our children to private Christian schools (or home school them), they live in a different world than we grew up in. They have more access to other perspectives than we had growing up. Most will go to college or live away from home by age eighteen. There is a real advantage to exposing children to diversity of thought when they are still living at home, under the supervision of parents.

Dealing with diversity of viewpoint on the gay issue within a local church provides parents with an opportunity to help their children find their way in such a world. We already practice this on other issues. A child may know an influential adult who is remarried after divorce and ask a parent, "Could you divorce daddy like Mrs. Jones did?" A parent might answer, "Even though Mrs. Jones is a wonderful person, she made a mistake in getting divorced. But we love and accept her anyway." We can love and admire people whose life decisions we don't agree with.

Parents who are conservative on the gay issue may think that exposure to respected gay adults will increase the likelihood that their children will choose to be gay themselves. There's simply no evidence that this is the case. The vast majority of people who identify as gay do so because they experience strong same-sex attraction, often in the absence of heterosexual attraction. Some adolescents (not many) may be unsettled about their sexual orientation for a time. But they need the wisdom and supervision of parents who set clear boundaries on sexual activity (gay or straight) during this period anyway.

And the simple fact is this: our children will not be nearly as focused on the gay issue as we are. This is true even of young people raised in conservative homes today. I've had so many of them tell me, "We are so over it. This is your issue to deal with, not ours." If anything, younger people—including from conservative families—increasingly disaffiliate from the church over exclusionary policies. As today's children get older, being in a church that singles gay people out for exclusion or disqualification from ministry will likely become an obstacle rather than a support to their faith.

A third way challenges liberals to refrain from holding conservatives in contempt (or mild condescension, as the case may be.)

The "liberal" is challenged to accept the "conservative," by not despising the conservative's scruples as unenlightened. Each person's choices within the framework of the narrow dispute are respected as decisions they make unto the Lord and for which they are answerable to the Lord. In particular, the liberal is challenged to accept and respect the choices that conservatives make on this question. They agree not to seek to undermine these choices. In particular, they agree to respect the choice of someone who seeks to change his or her same-sex orientation, to live celibate by conviction, or to marry.

Often the "liberal" is moved by a strong sense of justice. Living in a community in which everyone does not agree with the choices of gay brothers and sisters may seem like an injustice. These parents may worry that a conservative family's approach might negatively affect one of their own children who might come out as gay. They will be challenged to wrestle with the nature of the gospel: does the gospel call for affirmation of lifestyle or acceptance of the person despite objections over lifestyle questions? Does the moral approval we grant each other empower a deeper relationship than the gospel affords?

The "liberal" is called to practice restraint in their attitude toward the "conservative." Society models a different approach: it nurtures a posture of contempt, disdain, and dismissal toward the conservative. This leads to various forms of separation, distance, and alienation. The liberal in the third way approach is called to trade the pleasure of sharing faith in a like-minded group for the challenge of sharing faith in a diverse one. The liberal's instinctive commitment to diversity will be tested under the third-way approach.

A third way invites liberals and conservatives to redirect the energy that animates their moral concern over this issue to the Lord.

Both "liberal" and "conservative" are called to take the energy of their respective moral concerns and redirect it from "the issue at hand" to "the judge who is standing at the door." Consider Romans 14:10-12: "But why do you judge your brother? or why do you look down on your brother? for we shall all stand before the judgment seat of Christ. For it is written, As I live, said the Lord, every knee shall bow to me, and every tongue shall confess to God. So then every one of us shall give account of himself to God."

Today's Christians don't often appreciate the biblical doctrine of the resurrection as directly linked to the final judgment. In biblical thought, the doctrine of the resurrection at the last days came first. The resurrection of Jesus builds on this foundational understanding. When Jesus rose from the dead, he signaled the nearness of the coming judgment. Furthermore, in biblical thought, God does his saving as a judge—just as in Hebrew society a judge saved the poor from the oppression by judging the oppressor. To confess the risen Jesus, then, is to believe that the Judge is standing at the door. To use the language of James: "Grudge not one against another, brethren, lest you be condemned: behold, the judge stands at the door." (James 5:9)

Within the Vineyard, I learned to honor the role of experience. The more we experience the nearness of the Risen Jesus, the easier it is to leave the judging to him, knowing that he is standing at the door. Conversely, if our experience of Jesus is remote, the more tempted we are to fall into the trap of illicit judging. We may not call it that. We may call it instead, separating for the sake of righteousness, purity, or principle. Either way, God will be the judge.

Both "liberal" and "conservative" are called to take the energy of our moral objections and redirect it from "the issue" to our gospel obligation: to accept one another as Christ has accepted us.

A third way highlights the power of acceptance over the power of affirmation.

For Paul, the crux of the gospel is this: "For when we were yet without strength, in due time Christ died for the ungodly. For scarcely for a righteous man will one die: yet peradventure for a good man some would even dare to die. But God commendeth his love toward us, in that, while we were yet sinners, Christ died for us." (Romans 5:6-8).

When Jesus did this for us, he conferred on us a solemn obligation: to accept fellow sinners as God in Christ accepted us.

Paul's word is acceptance. "Him that is weak in the faith receive, but not to doubtful disputations ... for God has received him…. Wherefore receive one another, as Christ also received us to the glory of God." (Romans 14:1, 3; 15:7)

The focus is acceptance, not affirmation. Does our relationship hinge on our capacity to give or to gain the affirmation of each other? Over what? If over one aspect of our lifestyle, why not another? Where does a focus on affirmation lead us, into the heart of the gospel or away from the heart of the gospel?

It is understandable that in order to welcome those who were previously condemned, we might gravitate to the language of affirmation. When faced with a choice between condemning people or affirming them, we might say, "It's better to affirm them." I wouldn't argue with that.

But I want to linger on this point to consider the underlying assumptions behind the language of affirmation. There is a presumption at work in this language—that we are called as Christians to offer one another our moral approval as a sign of our acceptance. (By "affirming," I think we mean something like, "grant moral approval".) But maybe the granting or withholding of moral approval isn't a particularly Christian thing to do. Not just for covenanted gay couples, but for covenanted straight couples—for anyone, anywhere within the influence of the gospel.

The focus on affirmation is, I think, a reflection of our contemporary elevation of marriage (relative to the New Testament). With all our focus on defending marriage, an institution that we perceive to be under assault from many quarters, we have given marriage a kind of "pride of place" within the Christian community that it was never designed (by God) to occupy. We sometimes even name our churches, "Family Worship Centers." Which seems very family friendly, but if you're a single person, you don't think: "I belong in a church like that because after all, I'm part of a family too." You think, "This is a church that prefers to have couples with kids."

In other words, the church in recent decades has drifted into granting married couples a kind of "moral privilege." *These are the people who are doing it right.* I'm not saying anyone would assert or defend that statement explicitly. I'm saying it seems to have become a kind of under-the-radar-cultural posture within the church. Married people, in other words, seem to have been given the moral approval of the Christian community, categorically.

None of this is rooted in the gospel. I hasten to add that we can honor and bless each other without framing it as an act of moral approval. I feel a need to say that I was married to one woman for forty-two years, never had sex with anyone else but her, and she was the (let me count) second (possibly the third) non-related female I had ever kissed. And together we worked very hard to support people who are married in the sometimes-challenging task of staying married, an effort I plan to continue.

So why this reluctance, on my part, to adopt the language of affirmation, which I take to mean granting moral approval?

Because we are people of the gospel.

When we, even with the best of intentions, decide it is important—as an act of our faith—to grant moral approval to each other, we are not standing in the space cleared for us by the gospel. We are saying, by implication, that we belong to each other, we are "right with each other" because we grant each other moral approval.

And now to bring it into the realm of theology: When we do that, we're not eating from the tree of life, that tree freely given to us by a gracious God. We are eating, instead, from the tree of the knowledge of good and evil, the tree that was forbidden to us by the same gracious God, because its fruit in our lives would not be good. By eating this fruit, despite the prohibition, we have come to regard ourselves not as children following the leading of our Parent-God in all our doings, but as moral arbiters—the knowers of good and evil—who consider it our job, our religious duty even, to approve and condemn, like a judge. Like God.

It was the Pharisees, not Jesus, who believed that the granting or withholding of moral approval was a sacred obligation of the religious life. In the gospels, "a certain ruler" gave Jesus his moral approval by saying, "Good teacher!" It seemed an innocent enough greeting. Except that it wasn't at all innocent. It was the opposite of innocent. It was the greeting of the religious person eating from the tree of the knowledge of good and evil, as we sinners are wont to do. So, strangely to our ears, counter to our intuition, Jesus rejected this expression of moral approval by saying, "No one is good but God alone!" (see Luke 18:9-14).

This is a mysterious exchange, but I think there is solid theological justification to suggest that it may have been Jesus' way of saying, "You are involved in the wrong project: granting or withholding your moral approval of other human beings as if that were your religious duty. I'm calling you to abandon that project and take on my project. My project involves eating from the tree of life, not the tree of the knowledge of good and evil that so concerns you."

To shift metaphors, moral approval is the porridge—the cheap gruel—that we have exchanged for the birthright of the new creation, which is the acceptance afforded us in the gospel.

Of course, anyone is free to grant moral approval to anyone they wish. But let's not pretend that when we are doing this to each other or seeking this from each other—least of all viewing it as a distinctively Christian act—that we are standing on the firm ground of the gospel.

There is something more powerful that the gospel calls us to give each other: not affirmation, not moral approval, but acceptance.

Another word for acceptance is embrace. [124] The opposite of exclusion is not mere tolerance, but embrace. [125] The "other" is received as one who is beloved. [126]

---

124 Several commentators echo Dunn on the meaning of "accept" as "to receive or accept into one's society, home, circle of acquaintances." Dunn, p. 798.

125 See Volf, Miroslav. *Exclusion and Embrace: A Theological Exploration of Identity, Otherness and Reconciliation.* Nashville, Tenn.: Abingdon Press, 1996. pp.140-147 The Drama of Embrace. The people I know who are gay, the friends and the members of our church family, the couples, the families, are not people I "tolerate." They are people I embrace, bless, honor, receive, delight in.

126 Dunn, *Word Biblical Commentary*, p. 798.

Affirmation is about awarding or rendering a positive judgment concerning the other. This has become a very popular word from its use in the self-esteem movement. It is a fine word, but it's not a gospel word. Embrace is a gospel word.

Significant research on marriage reveals that core differences between married couples are rarely resolved. Instead couples who sustain a lifelong commitment are those who find a way to honor and respect each other anyway, avoiding the toxic forms of argument (which include criticism of character, contempt, defensiveness and stonewalling). [127] The beauty of the older married couple is in their hard fought acceptance of each other despite core differences. This is the beauty of the gospel as Paul applies the gospel in Romans 14-15.

Two Brothers, One House

After preparing this letter, I learned of two books by men who were raised as evangelical Christians (and embraced their faith as adults) telling two different stories about being gay. In *Washed and Waiting*, Wesley Hill writes of coming to understand his same-sex attraction as a disordered aspect of his life that is not likely to change. Out of faithfulness to Christ, he has chosen to remain celibate. [128]

In *Torn: Rescuing the Gospel from the Gay vs. Christian Debates*, Justin Lee, also a deeply devoted believer in Jesus, tells a slightly different story. Growing up with strong same-sex attraction (in the absence of any heterosexual desire), he pursued healing from same-sex orientation for years, and eventually became suicidal. After much prayer, soul-searching

---

127 Gottman, John and Silver, Nan. *The Seven Principles for Making Marriage Work*. New York, N.Y.: Three Rivers Press, 1999. pp 27-34

128 Hill, Wesley and Greene McCreight, Kathryn. *Washed and Waiting: Reflections on Christian Faithfulness and Homosexuality*. Grand Rapids, Mich.: Zondervan, 2012.

and study of Scripture, he is convinced that he can enter a same-sex union in faithfulness to Christ and Scripture. [129]

Both men are making their decisions with great concern for Christ, for the church, and for the inspiration of Scripture. They intend to live by their convictions "as unto the Lord."

What are we to make of their different stories? Both seem credible. Both seem driven by Christ-honoring motives. Any parent would be proud to have these two men as sons. One cannot but think that both are brothers in the family headed by the God and Father of our Lord Jesus Christ. Is one mistaken and the other correct? Is one building his life in Christ (and by extension, part of the temple of Christ's body on earth) with precious materials built to last, while another is building with wood, straw, and stubble? Is it possible that each is following the lead of the Spirit? A third-way approach is willing to allow these convictions to co-exist in the church as a way to honor the power of the gospel to create a firm foundation of unity in the face of this and even greater differences of conviction. In doing so we confess that God will save and God will judge and "The day will bring it to light."

In the meantime, we are called to practice the gospel discipline, the gospel glory, the gospel *enactment*, of mutual acceptance.

One can only feel the power of acceptance when one is on the receiving end of it, and there's nothing like it in heaven or on earth! This is a love that defies logic, explanation, even doctrinal formulation. It is jaw-dropping, shut-my-mouth! what-do-I-know about anything? wonder-love. A love we kneel before and sing about when discourse fails.

The only fitting response to this gospel is worship. It is not by accident that Paul closes his exhortation in Romans 14-15 with a prayer leading into a fugue of worship.

"Therefore receive one another, as Christ also received us to the glory of God. Now I say that Jesus Christ was a minister of

---

129 Lee, Justin. *Torn: Rescuing the Gospel from the Gay Vs. Christians Debate*. New York, N.Y.: Jericho Books, 2012.

the circumcision for the truth of God, to confirm the promises made unto the fathers: And that the Gentiles might glorify God for his mercy; as it is written, For this cause I will confess to you among the Gentiles, and sing to your name. And again he said, Rejoice, you Gentiles, with his people. And again, Praise the Lord, all you Gentiles; and laud him, all you people. And again, Esaias said, There shall be a root of Jesse, and he that shall rise to reign over the Gentiles; in him shall the Gentiles trust. Now the God of hope fill you with all joy and peace in believing, that you may abound in hope, through the power of the Holy Ghost." (Romans 15: 7-13)

The worship is not the song only or the words of praise. The worship is the act of accepting one another out of reverence for Christ. This reverie of worship is a sign that his exhortation to the Romans to accept one another in the face of the controversy raging among them, controversies involving their understanding of Scripture and what many would consider first order moral issues that divide them, was a fitting climax to his magisterial letter.

This is Paul functioning in his priestly role as Apostle to the Gentiles on behalf of the God of Israel. Here we see Paul making of the Roman church an offering to God, pleasing and acceptable—his act of spiritual worship. Paul is functioning here as an embodiment of Israel, God's royal priesthood, who in turn represents the priestly vocation of all humanity. We are to offer ourselves in all our vast diversity—Jew and Gentile, slave and free, male and female, along with all the differing perspectives that such categorical differences bring—as one people under God. Together we are holy, pleasing, acceptable. Together we belong to God, by virtue and for the sake of Christ. We freely offer ourselves, together only by virtue of and for the sake of Christ, to God.

For the Greater Glory of God and the Well-being of People

I began by saying that my approach to discernment has been shaped by the Ignatian framework. Ignatius taught that discernment is reserved for a choice between two goods. If the choice is between a good option and an evil option, then no discernment is needed. Choose the good, shun the evil.

I have attempted to show that the limited question of how to respond to gay and lesbian people who are seeking to form faithful-for-life partnerships, is an example of what St. Paul called "a disputable matter." This understanding opens the way to embrace gay and lesbian people who are seeking to follow Christ as full participants in the Christian community.

If this is correct, then the choice faced by those who disapprove of such relationships and those who approve of them is between the following two potential goods. These two goods are: 1) the good represented by the ultimate correctness of their position, and 2) the good of bearing witness to the Lordship of Jesus and his power to maintain a unity of the Spirit despite significant moral differences like this. [130]

Since Paul urges both "the weak" and "the strong" to honor their own conscience on this matter, [131] it is helpful to appreciate the potential good of each position. The rejection of all homosexual acts is rooted in a desire to uphold [132] what is understood to be the meaning of the prohibitive Scriptures and the tradition of heterosexual marriage. It is an attempt to be careful to walk in faithfulness to God. The rejection of exclusionary practices aimed at gay and lesbian people is rooted in a desire to uphold Scripture by seeking to carefully understand its meaning in the original historical context and to apply Scripture's teaching carefully. It is an attempt to uphold Scripture's caution against religious zeal

---

130 I am grateful to Rick Rykowski, the director of our Ignatian Spiritual Direction Training Program, for pointing this out to me.

131 Jewett, intriguingly and persuasively links this to Paul's use of terms like "measure of faith" and "gift of faith" in Romans 12-15. *See Christian Tolerance*, pp. 63-65

132 I beg the reader's indulgence in my characterization of these two positions. My intention is to offer a fair and sympathetic rendering of each.

that unintentionally accepts harm of the neighbor or fails to love the neighbor well. Both positions are principled positions seeking to uphold important goods.

While respecting the conscience of each group (and urging them to do the same) Paul points out a greater good: accept each other as Christ has accepted us. And do so as a prophetic sign of the power of the gospel to hold a kingdom with diverse and disparate cultures together in anticipation of the coming kingdom of God, in which God will be all in all. He asks each party to exercise enormous restraint for the sake of this greater good. This greater good is tied to what can be viewed as Paul's consistent life theme: he does what he does, advocates what he advocates, suffers what he suffers, for the sake of the gospel which has so gripped him and which he has done his best to reveal in his letter to the Romans.

Ignatius taught that the *ultimate* goal of any discernment process is to choose the option that is "for the greater glory of God and the well-being of people."

The gospel reveals the glory of God. It is the glory of God to do us good—to enter the human experience and effect a remarkable reconciliation with sinners through the power of acceptance. The third way, I believe, reveals the glory of the gospel as it pertains to one of our most contentious controversies. It does so in a way that is prophetic: that speaks to a deep need in our wearingly polarized society in a way that only the gospel can.

And the third way is for the well-being of people. Everyone, that is.

It affords space in churches for people who are gay, lesbian and transgender to pursue Christ. We are new at welcoming people who are gay, lesbian, and transgender into our church community in this way, but the people we have welcomed are grateful. They thank me personally, and earnestly, sometimes with tears because of the good that has come to them from being able to find Jesus in a church family. A friend who pastors a church that practices exclusion confided in me recently, "I have to admit, Ken, that if I had a child who was gay, I'd want them to find their way to your church." This is for the well-being of people.

When I spoke to a group of pastors and lay leaders on this approach recently, people who had gay and lesbian loved ones grabbed me by the arms and said words to this effect: "Thank you for giving me a way to love my loved ones who are gay and lesbian. This has been such a painful issue for me. It was tearing me up inside, and tearing our family up. I feel as though you've given me a path to freedom."

We gathered a group of people in the church to read and discuss an earlier version of this manuscript and a few related books. I asked them to share how this issue has affected them personally. We were all surprised to learn that it was a significant issue for every single person because each of them had a poignant story to tell about a friend or a family member who was gay. In every case, the controversy in the wider church over this issue was a major source of distress. Most had never talked about this before in a church setting.

Whether or not we are gay or have loved ones who are gay, many of us are torn up over this issue. We're anxious and fearful because we are afraid of losing relationships over this controversy. Those who believe all homosexual acts are wrong fear they will lose standing with those who see it differently. Those who believe that it is wrong to exclude people over this fear that others, who see it as a holiness issue, will reject them. People are afraid that if they change their position on this litmus test question, others in their family or close circle of friend will be scandalized.

Where does this anxiety come from? Much of it comes from the fear that our relationships with people we care about will suffer. It comes, more precisely, from our fear that we won't be accepted by those who disagree with us. *Our* belonging will be threatened. The gospel imperative to accept each other despite our differences over disputable matters is very good news indeed, if we walk in it. It's *good for us*. It's a relief to let go of all the pressure that comes with having to judge this matter correctly. It's a relief to know that we can hold to our own convictions without our belonging being threatened.

And if there *is* a way to deal with this controversial issue that doesn't require us to separate from each other, maybe we don't have to fear the next big controversial issue. Maybe we could happily get on with the exciting, satisfying and meaningful adventure that comes with following Jesus in the company of others who have experienced the soul-mending power of being accepted by Jesus. This is for the glory of God and the well-being of people. It is for our good—all of us, together.

CHAPTER 6

Yes, But This Is a *BIG* Change

THE GAY CONTROVERSY stirs such an array of passions because smack dab in the middle of it we find the institution of marriage. And we all have a stake in marriage.

Many of us grew up in homes torn apart by divorce. Facing our own marital struggles, we feel how fragile a thing a marriage can be. Living happily ever after with one other person for a lifetime that lasts much longer than was the case even a hundred years ago. … Whose idea was this anyway?

Things that touch on marriage are often touching a very raw nerve. Which means marriage, for better or worse, is the stuff of religion.

You can probably appreciate why I'd want us to step back for a little perspective. Especially when it's getting time to say how I would respond to a gay couple in love, hoping to dedicate their union to Jesus, seeking his help to keep their new family together.

And I do. I surely do want to step back for some perspective. It's as though I've been handed a ball of string all knotted up and it's my job to help untangle it. What do I do, but start to loosen one little knotted place at a time?

I'll begin where I began by honestly and rigorously considering the moral dilemmas that I faced when I engaged the previous religious controversy concerning marriage, the question of the legitimacy of remarriage after divorce. We've forgotten how intense that controversy was in its hey-day now that it has died down. But we have been here before, and not too long ago. Then I'll consider the very real challenges that confront people when lifelong celibacy (with no hope of change) is presented to them as the only faithful option. Finally, I'll invite us to consider how varied an institution marriage has been over the centuries, how many profound changes it has undergone before, during, and after the period when the writers of Scripture were addressing their concerns about marriage under the inspiration of the Holy Spirit. Because all of these issues are tightly bound together in this ball of knotted string called the gay controversy.

Does the "Definition of Marriage" Settle This Controversy?

After conferring with countless pastor colleagues and well-informed lay people about my changing views on the care of gay people in the church, I've learned that many do not dispute the fact that the handful of biblical texts that condemn same-sex relations have big interpretive challenges attached to them. But they offer a ready response that seems to make the problems of interpreting and applying the prohibitive texts moot. It goes like this: "I suppose there may be some issues there, but we know that sex outside of marriage is wrong and the Bible defines marriage as between one man and one woman. Same-sex relationships are immoral because they are extramarital."

Let's consider that. How does the biblical understanding of marriage inform one's view of the morality of same-sex relationships? Does the biblical definition of marriage settle the question once and for all? It's a potent argument for its simplicity. But it didn't settle the matter for me.

It did not resolve the pastoral dilemma I faced with people who wanted to remarry despite the biblical injunctions against remarriage in most cases. That's an important phrase, "the biblical injunctions against remarriage in most cases." Not too long ago, the church was convinced that remarriage after divorce was not allowed in most, if not all, cases. This was on the grounds that the Bible defined marriage as a permanent union that could not be broken, except by the death of a spouse (or later in the tradition, by one or two very narrow exceptions). Anyone—or most everyone—who remarried after divorce was by definition in an extramarital relationship because their first marriage was not dissolved in the eyes of God.

This same argument is used to condemn monogamous gay unions today. Even if the handful of prohibitive texts are not as clear as we once thought, given a very different historical context that may have been addressing different concerns, the biblical definition of marriage rules out gay unions. Or so it is frequently and confidently asserted.

We Can't Have it Both Ways

Thanks to our historical amnesia, we sometimes act as though remarriage after divorce is in a different moral universe than gay relationships. But is it? I began pastoral ministry in a very unusual church setting. In the 1980s, our church was almost exclusively composed of idealist young people who were either single or newly married. We were ardently focused, as only the idealist young can be, on doing everything right, and quite willing to dismiss the experience of our "compromising" elders. It was plain to us that Jesus ruled out most, if not all, remarriages, and he did so by defining marriage in a certain way. At least this was his ideal [133] or

---

133 "Ideal" seems to me to be a uniquely unbiblical word in the context of morality. The incarnate God seems rather to deal with the real, not some ideal, "ideal" being a concept that seems more Greek than Hebraic.

"the way it was meant to be originally." And as an idealistic young pastor, that settled it for me, and my experience didn't challenge my views. Most pastors have acted as though that biblical definition of marriage—marriage as an indissoluble union—does not settle the matter. In fact, virtually every church tradition, by theology, interpretive strategies, or pastoral practice, makes accommodations for divorced people who seek to remarry. These accommodations permit divorced people to enter unions that are outside the rule laid down in the Bible.

But we can't have it both ways. We can't apply a strict "biblical marriage" rule to gay people and not apply it to those who are divorced and remarried.

In order to appreciate my concern, I have to unpack the dilemma that a pastor faces when applying the "biblical definition of marriage" to divorced people seeking remarriage. This involves appreciating the tough questions that fueled the previous controversy as though we were facing it today.

You will be tempted to tune out of these details. We like our religion simple. But life is not simple. And have you read the Bible? Not a simple book.

I must caution readers who are remarried after divorce. These are painful texts to consider. But the pain that divorced and remarried people feel upon reading these texts is precisely the same pain that people who are in monogamous gay unions face reading the prohibitive texts treated earlier in this letter. We cannot be sensitive to the pain of one group while ignoring the pain of the other, especially when the other group (people who are gay, lesbian, and transgender) are a vulnerable minority within the general population. To do so would be to violate the justice of a just God.

Let's face these difficult texts together. Why was the church so reluctant to allow remarriage after divorce?

In Matthew 19, Jesus was asked a question about divorce. It's worth noting that Jesus didn't decide to stress the importance of marriage because he was on a campaign to

defend marriage against assault. He was responding to a
question about the lawful grounds for divorce, presented by
the Pharisees, who liked to pepper him with questions about
the controversial issues of their day. They weren't looking for
an answer so much as hoping to expose vulnerabilities in this
young, untrained rabbi's teaching.

Jesus responds by offering his interpretation of the Genesis
account: "at the beginning the creator made them male and
female" and said, "For this cause shall a man leave father
and mother, and shall cleave to his wife: and they two shall
be one flesh." (Matthew 19: 4-5) Then Jesus adds his own
commentary, saying, "Wherefore they are no more two, but
one flesh. What therefore God has joined together, let not man
put asunder." (Matthew 19: 6)

In other words, when Jesus is asked a question about the
proper grounds for divorce, he answers by saying something
about the permanence or indissolubility of marriage. Is
marriage permanent or temporary? When we divorce, is it
dissolved in God's eyes, or are we still married to the original
spouse no matter what the divorce courts say? That's an
important question. Practically speaking, morally speaking,
it's as important as whether people of the same gender can
enter covenantal unions like marriage.

Jesus defined marriage as a lifelong union that cannot be
dissolved (or at most, can only be dissolved in one particular
situation). For centuries, the church turned this definition
into a rule: no remarriage after divorce. The church wasn't
just being mean, it was being biblical: according to Jesus, the
person who remarries after divorce becomes an adulterer.
Why? They are having sex with someone who is not, in the
eyes of God, their spouse. They are having "sex outside of
marriage."

We've made so many pastoral accommodations in the
matter of remarriage (in many cases, correctly, I think) that
we've lost a sense for the strictness of this teaching. It wasn't

lost on the disciples who said, "If this is the case, it's better not to marry!"

This view of marriage as a lifelong relationship that cannot be broken to form another union is affirmed elsewhere in Scripture.

"And if a woman shall put away her husband, and be married to another, she commits adultery." (Mark 10: 12)

"Whosoever puts away his wife, and marries another, commits adultery: and whosoever marries her that is put away from her husband commits adultery." (Luke 16:18)

"The wife is bound by the law as long as her husband lives; but if her husband dies, she is at liberty to be married to whom she will; only in the Lord." (1 Corinthians 7:39)

"For the woman who has a husband is bound by the law to her husband so long as he lives; but if the husband dies, she is loosed from the law of her husband. So then if, while her husband lives, she marries another man, she shall be called an adulteress: but if her husband dies, she is free from that law; so that she is no adulteress, though she is married to another man." (Romans 7:2-3)

I can only imagine that readers may be wincing as I review this biblical material. We tend not to state this teaching so sharply out of concern to not "beat up" on people we know and love who are divorced. But we have to acknowledge what the Bible is saying here. The moral concern raised by the "no remarriage after divorce rule" is clear: when a divorced person remarries they enter a relationship that is immoral. This is precisely the argument used to rule out gay unions.

Pastors who care for divorced people seeking to marry again know that we don't say: "That settles it. You emptied your bed by getting divorced. Now sleep in it. You are never free to remarry, except to return to your original mate."

We don't, when we don't, because it feels cruel. We think it may be unbearable for many people.

We look for ways to make accommodations for the difficult circumstances of the people we know and love in light of what seems to be the plain teaching of Scripture regarding marriage.

We turn to Matthew 19: 9. Here Jesus says, "And I say unto you, whoever shall put away his wife, except it be for fornication, and shall marry another, commits adultery: and whoever marries her which is put away commits adultery." So maybe there is at least one exception (and if there is one, perhaps more can be found in Scripture). When a person whose spouse commits adultery is divorced, the "innocent" party is free to remarry, because the adultery dissolved the original union. Faced with people in deep anguish after divorce that have found someone to love, we pastors are *happy* to find an exception and we hope it applies because we're reluctant to lay burdens on people that they cannot carry.

When pastors are conscientious, they try to understand what the exception is and how it applies. Let's not open a hole in the Bible that we can drive a Mack truck through. In fact, the text doesn't open a very large hole at all. It may simply allow for divorce while remaining silent with respect to remarriage. We have to *infer* that the exception for divorce applies to the freedom to remarry. Many dispute this inference, and not without grounds. The largest and oldest Christian tradition says that it only confers the freedom to divorce, not to remarry. Catholics wisely claim that when a text of Scripture is not clear, it should be interpreted in light of texts that are clear. All the other sayings of Jesus make no reference to any possible exceptions. They seem very clear. Consider these two texts again, paying attention to the highlighted words.

"If a woman shall put away her husband, and be married to another, she commits adultery." (Mark 10: 12)

"*Whosoever* puts away his wife, and marries another, commits adultery: and whosoever marries her that is put away from her husband commits adultery." (Luke 16:18)

These seem like sweeping and clear statements that leave no room for exceptions.

A debate ensues over what this one possible exception may refer to:

"Whoever divorces his wife, except in the case of sexual immorality, and marries another, commits adultery." (Matthew 19: 9)

When considering the one possible exception, we try to understand what "sexual immorality" refers to. We look at the word in the original Greek. We may even wonder what the actual word that Jesus used (in Aramaic) might have been. The Greek turns out to be a more general term, *pornea*, whose meaning isn't precise. (The root of the word is related to sex for sale.) The debate is on. Does the exception mean that if your spouse has a one-night stand and repents, you're still free to divorce? Does it mean that if your spouse has a pornography problem, you're free to divorce? What if you *both* have a pornography problem? And even if it is established that you are free to divorce, are you free to remarry? What if you are the one who had the affair and now you've repented, but in the meantime, the affair led to divorce? Are you free to remarry since you've repented? Where is that clear in the so-called exception?

It turns out that interpreting and then applying this exception to the rule—if it's meant to serve as a rule—is very difficult.

We pastors, faced with a steady stream of hard cases, look for other exceptions to this very hard teaching in the Bible. And we find a candidate in 1 Corinthians 7:15-16: "But if the unbelieving depart, let him depart. A brother or a sister is not under bondage in such cases: but God has called us to peace. For how do you know, O wife, whether you shall save your husband? Or how do you know, O man, whether you shall save your wife?"

We find the same kinds of ambiguities with this exception and we have the same kinds of debates. What does Paul mean by "not bound"? Not bound to stay married even though the unbeliever has left? Or free to remarry—a bigger step, since the unbeliever might return, and then what? We debate [134] the meaning of the Greek in this context, and what light might be shed by "God has called us to peace" and so on.

There is a cottage industry of Christian books devoted to this debate. They don't sell as well as they used to because it's not as controversial an issue in our day as it was even thirty years ago. Most churches have resolved the difficulty by making rather generous accommodations. In my own denomination, remarriage is rarely regarded as a reason to categorically disqualify someone from membership or any form of leadership. There's never been a hue and cry for our national leadership to address the issue, despite the fact that divorce is a serious issue affecting untold numbers of people in the denomination.

The Roman Catholic Church, which takes the strictest view, makes considerable accommodations through the annulment process. If a divorced Catholic wants the blessing of the church to marry again, they apply for an annulment. The church investigates whether the marriage was a legitimate one in the first place. In the early years of the church, grounds for declaring that a true marriage never existed were very narrow. They included things like a person married under threat of violence, or a person married his half sister without knowing it, or the marriage was never consummated. The grounds for annulment have expanded dramatically over time. What did the parties intend or understand with respect to the purposes of marriage? Did both parties realize being married means being open to having children? In the 1990s, the Catholic church in the United States granted about 60,000 annulments

---

134 My point here is actually different. Often we don't engage in the debate any longer because the matter has been settled, if informally, by a different pastoral practice. I should say instead, "we rely on a consensus that followed a debate that most of us didn't engage in personally."

a year. [135] That number has since come down. Many more divorced Catholics than this don't even seek annulments from the church. They stop going to church and remarry. Or they go to another church and remarry. Perhaps the number of annulments would be even higher if more people applied for them. In the Catholic view, the annulment allows the person to enter a new marriage. This new marriage is not considered a second marriage because the first marriage was deemed invalid. Hence the term "annulment," not "divorce."

The vast array of Protestant churches take a different approach to making accommodations to the strict "no marriage after divorce" rule.

By the time of the Protestant Reformation, two exceptions to the strict "no remarriage after divorce" rule were thought to exist. The "innocent party" in a divorce caused by the adultery of a spouse—with debate still raging about whether the adultery is "one time" or "ongoing" or "ongoing for how long?"—is free to remarry. The guilty party is not free to do so. In addition, if a believer is married to an unbeliever (definitions are still under dispute) and the unbeliever deserts, the believer is free to remarry.

Any pastor knows that while these two exceptions help some divorced people to remarry, it seems there should be other exceptions as well. What about spousal physical abuse? What about extreme emotional abuse, something more difficult to define? The Bible doesn't cover these exceptions explicitly, so pastors just add them, or link them to one of the existing biblical exceptions (anyone who abuses another is no longer a believer and has, in effect, deserted his mate, etc.).

The longer a pastor is involved in pastoral ministry, the more exceptions seem to be reasonable. When one spouse has severe "narcissistic personality disorder," married life can become untenable. Or what of a spouse who develops alcoholism and refuses to get help, making life miserable for the family? Is this part of the "for better or worse, in sickness

---

135 http://www.divorcereform.org/rates.html

and in health" or is it grounds for divorce with freedom to remarry?

A pastor knows that different people have different capacities in these trying situations. Some can endure hardships that others cannot. I've known people who feel trapped in bad marriages and stay in these marriages only to become clinically depressed, even suicidal. They don't seem to be rebelling against carrying a cross that they are able to carry. This particular cross seems to be a burden they *can't* carry.

Within the Protestant tradition, the grounds for exceptions, in other words, expand for pastoral reasons, just as the Roman Catholic Church has expanded the grounds for annulment.

As a pastor dealing with these difficult situations, I completely understand this phenomenon. But it didn't happen until the divorce rate skyrocketed after World War II and churches were flooded with divorced people for whom the biblical teaching just seemed too strict to enforce. And pastors felt that it was harmful to insist on it, that it involved placing a burden on people that they weren't *able* to carry.

All this is not ancient history, either. As recently as 1957, the great Christian apologist, C.S. Lewis, wanted to marry a divorcee named Joy Davidman. Despite Lewis' contention that her previous marriage to an alcoholic and abusive husband had not been a true marriage, a bishop refused his request since it was contrary to canon law. A young cleric eventually performed the wedding because he prayed about it and felt Jesus would want him to. During the ceremony, he laid hands on the new Mrs. Lewis, who was suffering from bone cancer. She soon went into an unexpected remission. [136]

What the policy of the Church of England decreed with regard to the proposed marriage of C.S. Lewis to Joy Davidman—that it was illicit—most pastors wouldn't think to insist on today. We take the approach that the priest who

---

136 Jacobs, Alan. *The Narnian: The Life and Imagination of C.S. Lewis.* San Francisco, Calif.: Harper San Francisco, 2005. pp. 277-278

eventually performed the Lewis wedding took: we pray about it and do as we feel led by the Spirit to do.

This is what I have done. Along with my wife Nancy, I put a lot of pastoral care into helping marriages stay together despite major challenges. We did this especially with those who were committed to Christ and personally conscientious. Such work can be deeply satisfying when difficult marriages are saved and people go on to live more happily.

But some people aren't just conscientious. They are scrupulous. They remain in impossible situations too long. For all the "easy divorce" culture, there are such people and pastors care for them. Sometimes, though, looking back, I wish I had been more willing to simply say to a *few* such people, "This marriage is inflicting too much harm on everyone. We're in this with you. If you decide it's time to call it quits, that would be completely understandable. And I don't think it would consign you to a life of celibacy. You would be free to remarry." I am thinking of one respected member of our church, in particular. A few years ago, after she remarried a wonderful man, I told her that I wish I had been more supportive of her divorce earlier. If the reader thinks this means that I don't say such a thing to any married person without fear and trembling before God, then I've done a poor job conveying how Nancy and I, in our pastoral ministry, have fought for marriages.

I got to this place through *experience*—that word again. And it has forced me to ask the question, "Is the biblical teaching on marriage simply *descriptive*, that is, does it simply describe what marriage is meant to be as a norm? Or is it also *prescriptive*, that is, does it lay down clear rules that must be followed in every case? In my pastoral practice, I have answered that question. I have said, "It's God's original intention, in general, for people who marry to stay married for life. But that doesn't mean that people who are trapped in deeply harmful marriages must either remain married, or remain single after divorce. I've determined, by my pastoral practice, that it is legitimate to regard the text as *descriptive*, as generally normative, not *prescriptive*—that is, not prescribing what must happen in every case.

Even as I acknowledge this, I feel concerned. Does this pastoral accommodation so loosen the commitments made in marriage that more people will get divorced than really need to?

It probably makes it easier to divorce and remarry, that's hard to dispute. But is that good or bad? It all depends on the particular situation. If it's my daughter locked in a bad marriage, I don't want her to feel trapped. If someone without much loyalty goes through a rough patch in marriage, I'd prefer that they didn't feel so free to divorce.

Life is messy and marriage is in the middle of the mess, where pastors also do their best work. We can try to construct a mental map that eliminates the messiness. But these mental maps never account fully for the complexities of real life. Simply playing it safe by always erring in the direction of strictness—when in doubt assume that the Bible doesn't allow remarriage—may feel safe for us, but it can be dangerous for others. And if we place burdens on people that we are not willing (or, in the case of marriage, able) to help them carry, then we may, not to put too fine a point on it, have hell to pay. Jesus sternly warned his disciples not to do this. So we find our way forward, trusting in the kindness, goodness and mercy of God, just as much as divorced people facing remarriage must.

Now we face a similar challenge. Marriage with someone of the opposite sex is very difficult to maintain for people who have strong same-sex orientation. People with same-sex attraction have experienced this for a very long time, but the rest of us are becoming aware of it only in recent years. In the same way that the church didn't have to face the tough questions about divorce and remarriage until there was an increase in the divorce rate in the modern era, we haven't had to face the tough questions about same-sex relationships until they became more open in society. We didn't know about these struggles before because people who faced them couldn't share them openly without suffering more harm, without risking their lives in some cases.

For years, I bought the simple answer to this: "If you can't live in a heterosexual marriage, be celibate. People don't die just because they can't have sex."

The Limits of the Celibacy Solution

It's especially easy for a married pastor to say this, but we have to be thoughtful about the burdens we insist that *other* people carry, especially when we don't have to carry those same burdens ourselves.

Paul took this into account when he said, "Now concerning the things that you wrote to me about: It is good for a man not to touch a woman. Nevertheless, to avoid fornication, let every man have his own wife, and let every woman have her own husband." (1 Corinthians 7:1-2) It seems to me that Paul is not simply writing as an apostle here. He is writing as a pastor.

The church in our time has such an elevated view of marriage that we sometimes fail to hear Paul's words: "It is good for a man not to marry." In general, it's good not to marry, he says. As a matter or principle. Paul isn't coming up with this himself. He is echoing the emphasis of Jesus in Matthew 19: 10-12. [137]

Paul had no particular aversion to asking people to do hard things. But he was also realistic about what people *could* do. And Paul knew this particular Corinthian congregation. He knew what was happening: people were having sex. He knew that nature was tilted in this direction to ensure that God's first

---

137 His disciples said to him, If the case of the man be so with *his* wife, it is not good to marry. But he said unto them, All *men* cannot receive this saying, save *they* to whom it is given. For there are some eunuchs, which were so born from *their* mother's womb: and there are some eunuchs, which were made eunuchs of men: and there be eunuchs, which have made themselves eunuchs for the kingdom of heaven's sake. He that is able to receive *it*, let him receive *it*.

commandment (be fruitful and multiply and fill the earth) would be fulfilled. He doesn't lay a burden on people that he knows they are not able to carry. Perhaps Paul, a Pharisee, took to heart Jesus' rebuke of the Pharisees: "For they bind heavy burdens and grievous to be borne, and lay them on men's shoulders; but they themselves will not move them with one of their fingers." (Matthew 23:4)

We face the limits of our human capacity all the time. Pastors, especially, are aware of this, or ought to be. We make decisions with moral implications all the time, but we only *examine* those moral implications some of the time. The average middle class American, for example, uses perhaps four times more than their fair share of available resources. If everyone in the world owned as much stuff as we do, it would require four planets worth of stuff. By any reasonable measure, I think that would constitute what the Bible calls greed. Our average American lifestyle is greedy. Many have normalized to this and would deny that they are greedy people. Those who live on much less than their fair share in the developing world might be in a better position to judge. But even if one says, "Lord, have mercy! This is so wrong!" it is not easy to just stop using more than our fair share of energy and resources. Few people, when push comes to shove, are able to do it. We can make some improvements, but that just means we're less greedy. But we do not condemn such people. We don't exclude them from our churches or from any ministry in our churches. We are perhaps reflexively merciful to them because *they are us.*

So the plain fact is: we *do* take what people can do into account and we do it all the time.

Having raised five children through the sexual awakening of adolescence, my wife and I placed a *big* emphasis on deferring sexual intimacy until finding one's partner for life. Since we had sex too early and experienced the negative effects, this was more than a theoretical value for us. But in the process of repeatedly reinforcing "don't" when it comes

to sex (a legitimate concern) it was easy to lose sight of
the big-picture purpose of sex. These children are not just
sexual beings in order to have sex. They are sexual beings
to help them find a partner who can be a source of comfort,
consolation, and security through a life of suffering and
hardship, even into old age. Sex serves this other purpose,
as well as the purpose of procreation. People who find such
relationships thrive physically and emotionally as a result.
And the fact is: few relationships in modern society, including
the non-marital relationships fostered in churches, deliver on
this like marriage does.

It is one thing for a person to choose celibacy as a way to
honor God or because they don't experience the physical or
emotional needs that marriage fulfills. Or to choose celibacy
because they have been given the grace to flourish despite
those needs being unmet. It's one thing to delay marriage until
one finds a mate worth giving up one's independence for. It's
one thing to feel that it is taking far too long to find a mate.
But it is quite another, quite another thing altogether, to have
the burden of lifelong celibacy thrust on you (with no hope of
it ever being lifted) simply by virtue of your being gay, lesbian,
or transgender.

Many pastors don't seem to consider this. Something like
98 percent of Protestant clergy is married. The vast majority
is also heterosexual in orientation. In *A Moral Theology of the
New Testament*, Richard Hays, professor of New Testament at
Duke, says this: "While Paul regarded celibacy as a charisma,
he did not therefore suppose that those lacking the charisma
were free to indulge their sexual desires outside marriage.
Heterosexual persons are also called to abstinence from sex
unless they marry (1 Corinthians 7:8-9)."

Hays then goes on to say, "The only difference—admittedly
a salient one—in the case of homosexually oriented persons
is that they do not have the option of heterosexual 'marriage.'
So where does that leave them? It leaves them in precisely
the same situation as the heterosexual who would like to

marry but cannot find an appropriate partner (and there are many such): summoned to a difficult, costly obedience, while 'groaning' for the redemption of our bodies (Romans 8:23)."

Hays recognizes the "salient" difference that gay people don't have the option of heterosexual marriage. But then he makes the questionable assertion that this leaves homosexually oriented persons in "precisely the same situation" as the heterosexual who cannot find a suitable mate. There was a time, especially as a married pastor, when I might not have quibbled with Hays over this. But since then, my life circumstances have changed. I found myself at age 60, suddenly single after the death of my spouse. After less than a year of singleness, I started to feel the full weight of this. I began to feel the absence of a partner to share life with, someone I trusted deeply and could depend on because we had formed a deep pair bond. When I first started preparing this letter for publication, I didn't know if I would ever remarry. A Catholic friend suggested I start a monastic order for evangelicals. Later he suggested I consider the priesthood. I haven't taken him up on either. I like having the option—or at least the hope of marriage.

The hope, in a very real way, is the substance of the thing hoped for. The hope matters. Its absence, in the case of the gay person consigned to lifelong celibacy, *is* a salient difference that is *also* a substantial and significant one. This is *not* "precisely the same situation" as the heterosexual person who has not yet found a mate!

As a widower, how would I feel if the Christian teaching were simply: "marriage is for one woman and one man, one time, period"? No remarriage, even in the event of the death of a spouse. *This* would be equivalent to the situation faced by Hays' imagined homosexual person. Except that I enjoyed forty-two years of marriage to the woman of my dreams. According to the actuarial tables, I have about twenty years more to live (give or take.) My libido is not what it used to be. I suspect I'm more set in my ways than I used to be and I suppose I have a disincentive, compared to my younger self, to mold those ways to another.

And yet, even I can experience the reality that the hope really matters. If that is true for me, what of the young gay person who has never known what it means to be married and is anticipating sixty or seventy years without such a relationship? Someone who doesn't have the benefit of five wonderful children, many dear friends and a supportive church family?

For a long time, the answer to that concern has been to assure people that God can heal their same-sex orientation. But that promise has been vastly overstated. I know people who have successfully transitioned from experiencing same-sex attraction to having enough other-sex attraction to sustain a healthy and satisfying marriage relationship. Sexuality is a complex phenomenon and to think that it's absolutely fixed for everyone is, I think, more a product of ideology than biology. And yet, there are many for whom it is firmly fixed and not likely to change. Experience can change the brain, but there are limits to how much the brain can change. Some people can bear celibacy graciously. But others cannot. For them, the now traditional teaching that the biblical view of marriage—one man, one woman, for life— is descriptive but not prescriptive in the case of remarriage, is *absolutely prescriptive* in the case of gender. This means that it can *only ever* be for a man and a woman. Can we understand how that might constitute an unbearable burden?

Even if we were *willing* to do everything we can to assist them in carrying this burden, often we are not *able* to give them the help they really need. Because what they need is a companion, a partner, someone to cuddle with. Someone they can trust to be there for them through thick and thin.

As a Protestant, I can appreciate how the Catholic approach to remarriage, understood conscientiously, constitutes an unbearable burden. I have a friend who is a leader in the charismatic renewal that swept through the Roman

Catholic Church in the 1970s. My friend knows as many ardent, dedicated, committed and Spirit-empowered Roman Catholics as it is possible to know. We were recently discussing the Roman Catholic approach to remarriage. I was contending that the Roman Catholic annulment process is, in practice, equivalent to divorce. As a convinced Catholic, he objected, stating that Catholics whose marriages are annulled had never been truly married. He stated that many Catholics who have been divorced don't receive annulments because the question in granting an annulment is not "was this marriage extremely broken" but "was there a true marriage when the couple married?" He cited, as an example, the extreme case of a validly married person whose spouse became physically abusive later in the marriage. The good Catholic is free to separate, even divorce, but not to remarry so long as the original marriage was a valid marriage. The only option for the Catholic who wants to be faithful to church teaching is to remain single for life, or if they have remarried and are raising children, to live celibate within that second marriage, which is actually not a true marriage at all but an adulterous relationship if sex is involved.

I hope you are following the details here, because they matter when it comes to morality. They matter just as much as questions surrounding the morality of two gay people entering a lifelong union with a sexual dimension.

I challenged my Catholic friend (he challenges me just as sharply on other matters) with this question: Do you actually know any Catholics in this situation? Do you personally know any divorced Catholics who didn't qualify for an annulment, who subsequently remarried outside of the Catholic Church and now want to be faithful to Catholic teaching, and are currently living as brother and sister with their new spouse (who isn't a true spouse in the eyes of the Catholic church)? My friend admitted that he doesn't know a single person doing this. Which tells me this cannot be God's way. There would be more people able to do it, a lot more.

Just saying "celibacy is the solution" doesn't make it so. People have to be able to do it. Paul, a huge proponent of celibacy, knew this. The difficulty that divorced people have maintaining lifelong celibacy was part of the pastoral dilemma that forced us to take a closer look at our very restrictive policies regarding remarriage, policies that most contemporary pastors are unfamiliar with because it was the controversy of an earlier era.

It is in the nature of a good under-shepherd, a good pastor, to sympathize with the dilemmas faced by the people he or she cares for. We all owe this to each other. I have had to ask myself, "Is it right for me to insist that a certain class of people must live their lives without this possibility?" I have concluded that this is placing too great a burden on those in my care.

I am not arguing that the human authors of Scripture [138] anticipated modern-day faithful, loving, same-sex unions between equals and wanted to leave room for them in future generations when the issue finally came up. I don't think inspiration works that way. I don't think the human authors of Scripture anticipated what modern heterosexual married relationships have become, let alone gay relationships. Yet, that does not mean that Scripture forbids such relationships. It simply means that these texts of Scripture—including the texts of Scripture pertaining to marriage—do not address the question.

Not the First Big Marriage Controversy

The previous controversy about marriage—whether remarriage after divorce is ever possible, or possible in more circumstances than the very narrow (and hotly disputed) "biblical exceptions to then remarriage rule"—touched on the permanence of marriage.

---

138 It's a sad commentary on the intensity of this particular controversy that I feel a need to include a footnote that says to *my* friends: I also believe that Scripture has a divine author.

Today, our controversy has shifted to a new question, not the permanence of marriage but whether marriage as a union between a man and woman rules out the legitimacy of all same-sex acts, by definition. Marriage has been around for a long time and the question of gender hasn't been debated seriously until recently. But that fact doesn't mean the debate is not legitimate. When might it have come up earlier? When Aquinas, a doctor of the church, taught that homosexual acts were worse than incest? When the church commonly conflated the horrors of the attempted gang rape of the visitors to Sodom with all homosexual acts? Or when the church had no understanding or even recognition of the reality of same-sex orientation?

The church doesn't go looking for raging controversies. They come up when historical circumstances change and the issue is forced.

The question of whether Christians should go along with, support or even tolerate the institution of slavery didn't arise until *nearly eighteen centuries* after the gospel was announced. It didn't come up because it wasn't a real possibility. People couldn't imagine a world that worked without slavery. These things come up when the complex forces of history converge to bring them to our attention. Then we face them.

In the meantime, we shouldn't be naïve about marriage as if it is an unchanging institution, fixed throughout the centuries. As I read the biblical witness to marriage, I don't see a monolithic, unchanging institution. I see a patchwork of different arrangements over the centuries. The nature of marriage has changed in significant, even dramatic ways throughout the biblical era and throughout church history.

At times "biblical marriage" was endogamous (Abraham married his half sister); or polygamous (King David had more than one wife.) For the entire biblical period, family elders, often for economic reasons, selected marriage partners for their children. Today, this might be viewed as inconsistent with the consent necessary for legitimate marriage. The practice of "child marriage" was allowed in the biblical era. It was common for older men to marry younger women, including minors by today's standards. (Joseph and Mary may have been such a couple.) Today, this would be regarded as criminal abuse. During and after the biblical era women were regarded as property. This perspective is reflected in some biblical texts. Today, this would be considered slavery rather than marriage.

In the Greco-Roman world of Paul's mission, slaves were not allowed to marry. We don't know how the church handled this. They may have simply treated slaves who lived together as married. What did they do when slave couples were split up? Could slaves even "couple" in that sense? Were they allowed partners? Could they have sex as Christians under these circumstances? We don't know.

Long after monogamous marriage had become the norm, Christian missionaries met people who had more than one wife. Societies sometimes accept this practice when there are too few men to go around after war. Simply busting up the practice of polygamy had several harmful consequences, so some missionaries decided to accommodate the practice.

In other words, significant changes in the institution of marriage are par for the historical course. The question of gender, like the question of age, or the question of women as property, can reasonably be brought up for consideration. The only reason it can't be considered calmly, thoughtfully, and carefully—without people threatening to withdraw from Christian fellowship with each other over the question—is that we are surrounded by an intense atmosphere of controversy.

As I reflect on the gay marriage controversy, I see a great deal of hyperbolic fear clouding our thinking. I don't think gay unions will ever be anything but a minority arrangement. Sexual attraction is a key component in forming lifelong unions. The vast majority of people, some research suggests

as many as 94-97 percent, are heterosexually oriented. [139] .
Marriage between a man and a woman (and we should add,
"for life") can and should continue to be held in honor, whether
there are people who are faithful to each other in same-sex
covenantal unions. The existence of such unions for those
who would have great difficulty maintaining faithfulness in
heterosexual relationships due to their sexual orientation need
not undermine commitments heterosexual couples make to
each other.

The church at large didn't respond to the challenges that
divorced people face until divorced people came out of the
shadows and flooded the churches when the divorce rate rose
sharply in the wake of the Second World War. We're dealing
with the gay issue today because gay people are coming out
of hiding after being driven underground for centuries, in
part by distorted readings of Scripture promulgated by the
church. [140] So here we are. Today, more gay and lesbian people
are willing to be known. Those who know them are willing
to acknowledge them to others. Some are making their way
into our churches. Because they are few in number compared
to the ranks of the divorced, we can have successful churches
without them. If we are perceived to be too friendly to them,
we risk losing members who object to their presence. It is not
a recipe for an easy transition in local congregations, is it?

So what kind of considerations might we give, if we *were*
to be as sympathetic to the needs of gay people as we are
sympathetic to the needs of divorced people?

---

139 Gates, Gary J., *How many people are lesbian, gay, bisexual and
transgender?*, The Williams Institute, University of California School of
Law April 2001
140 I have in mind my earlier comments on the use of "sodomy" to
refer to all gay sex, based on what is now widely viewed as a distorted
reading of Genesis 19: 3-5.

Has the Gay Controversy Overheated Our View of Marriage?

I think we need to step back from the overheated controversy and get our bearings on how the kingdom of God, revealed in Jesus, influences our view of marriage in the first place. When we are as focused as the church is today on defending marriage against perceived attacks, we can forget that Jesus did not place a big emphasis on marriage. Jesus downgraded the significance of marriage compared to the Jewish perspective of his time. When the Scribes tried to trap him with questions about marriage in the new age, he said, "Not an issue. There is no marriage in the new age." In a time when marriage was expected of rabbis, Jesus didn't get married. He elevated the role of eunuchs (Matthew 19:11-12), people who were excluded from temple worship, according to the Law of Moses. Paul followed in his master's footsteps in de-emphasizing the significance of marriage. For Paul, marriage *itself* (and not just divorce) was a concession to human weakness (see 1 Corinthians 7:1-7).

I've often heard it said that marriage between a man and a woman is God's ideal. I don't think so. This flatly contradicts the teaching of Paul (with support from Jesus) that celibate singlehood is a higher call than marriage. If there is an "ideal" in Scripture, lifelong celibacy is it. Marriage is for those who can't cut it.

We're not used to hearing this biblical truth. Many of us were raised in the era of easy divorce. We understandably view the Bible as rushing to the defense of this embattled institution. And certainly, "the marriage bed" as the author of Hebrew says, "must be held in honor." But to honor something means that we must let it be what it is meant to be and not seek to make it more than that.

By elevating marriage, relative to the witness of the New Testament, we've loaded a great deal onto this institution. What began as a very practical arrangement, an economic one focused primarily on the care of children and the support of the extended family as a small business, became an institution entered by those in the throes of romantic love, understood in modern terms. It's difficult to find much emphasis on romantic love in earlier forms of marriage. Today married couples are expected to be each other's best friends, closest confidantes, trusted advisers, cheerleaders. Many men don't have a single male friend they can turn to in time of need. All of their social and relational needs—beyond the somewhat functional relationships at work—have to somehow be met by their wives. The pressure is just too much for one institution to bear!

Elevating marriage, which seems like a good thing, can actually be harmful to marriage. The more ambivalent New Testament perspective on marriage is helpful to consider as we try to understand what marriage can and cannot provide.

But there is also a deep theological basis for what might be viewed as a downgrade to the status of marriage. Marriage has to do with the age that is already passing away, now that Jesus has inaugurated the coming kingdom of God.

All this focus on marriage generated by intense, politically charged, media-incited controversy simply isn't in keeping with our identity as followers of a risen Lord who is bringing us a foretaste of the new age now. After all, in the gospels, the Pharisees, who were involved in their own controversies about marriage, brought up these questions. It's not as though marriage was a major plank in Jesus' messianic platform.

Sometimes this "coming kingdom logic" has been used to insist that gay people remain celibate for life with no hope of ever being married. Marriage isn't so important, so celibacy shouldn't be so hard. Fine. But let's apply that logic in an even-handed way. Let's apply it to divorced people who want to remarry despite the biblical prohibitions and lets apply it to single people who simply *want* to marry but don't *have* to in order to maintain sexual continence. Of course, we won't do that.

Instead, we might ask why the church is so preoccupied with a controversy about *marriage*, an institution that is part of the age that is passing away and has nothing to do with the age to come. Why are we raising the heat in this debate rather than lowering it? Paul reserved his heat for his concerns about the gospel itself, not things like marriage. Why are we separating over this as if our very identity in Christ were at stake?

The same can be said of gender. Simply put, gender is not the same concern it used to be, once the crucified Lord entered the new age and brought it back into the present for us to taste in advance. [141] Jesus undermined plenty of gender norms in his day, as did Paul. And Paul, who only knew the *Risen* Lord, radically de-emphasized the significance of gender differences when we said, "In Christ there is no male nor female." I'm not saying gender is no longer significant. I'm saying its significance seems to diminish as the kingdom of God nears.

What if we understood marriage as a concession to human weakness *for everyone* to whom it is given? There is plenty of biblical warrant for this view.

Jesus taught that Moses sanctioned divorce as a concession to human weakness (hardness of heart). [142] In the beginning,

---

141 By this, I do not mean to imply that I think issues pertaining to gender differences have been resolved. Gender justice concerns, for example, haven't suddenly abated.

142 Matthew 19:3-12 The Pharisees also came unto him, tempting him, and saying unto him, Is it lawful for a man to put away his wife for every cause? And he answered and said unto them, Have you not read, that he which made them at the beginning made them male and female, And said, For this cause shall a man leave father and mother, and shall cleave to his wife: and they two shall be one flesh? Wherefore they are no more two, but one flesh. What therefore God has joined together, let not man put asunder. They said to him, Why did Moses then command to give a writing of divorce, and to put her away? He said to them, Moses because of the hardness of your hearts suffered you to put away your wives: but from the beginning it was not so. And I say unto you, Whosoever shall put away his wife, except

he said, marriage formed a one-flesh union that shouldn't (or can't) be broken. The disciples were shocked by the implications of this: "If that's the case, it would be better not to marry!" Jesus didn't dispute this assertion. Rather, he said there were people who were called to forgo marriage, and those who could, should. In 1 Corinthians 7:1-2, [143] Paul is simply echoing Jesus in saying that marriage itself is a concession to human weakness.

Rather than exclude divorced people from the community, Moses provided a certificate of divorce, allowing for remarriage. Jesus argues that this was not God's original intent, but he doesn't indicate whether the Mosaic concession continues to be applicable for the same reasons it was instituted (the inability of some people in some situations to maintain lifelong commitment). At any rate, whether through expanded grounds for annulment or expanded grounds for divorce and remarriage, the church in her pastoral mode has made accommodations to the real challenges people face. Why shouldn't this apply, by analogy, to monogamous gay partnerships for those who are not able to live in a heterosexual marriage or in a state of celibacy? If marriage is given as a concession to weakness for *all* of us, perhaps it

---

it be for fornication, and shall marry another, commits adultery: and whoever marries her commits adultery. His disciples said to him, If the case of the man be so with his wife, it is not good to marry. But he said unto them, All men cannot receive this saying, save they to whom it is given. For there are some eunuchs, which were so born from their mother's womb: and there are some eunuchs, which were made eunuchs of men: and there be eunuchs, which have made themselves eunuchs for the kingdom of heaven's sake. He that is able to receive it, let him receive it.

143 Now concerning the things whereof you wrote unto me: *It is* good for a man not to touch a woman. Nevertheless, *to avoid* fornication, let every man have his own wife, and let every woman have her own husband.

should be granted as a concession to those among us who are gay, lesbian, and transgender.

One could say that I've gotten soft on this issue. I don't think that's because I'm looking for a way to avoid hard things in Scripture. I think there's a simple explanation. My views on this have been deeply affected by knowing, and now coming to love, gay couples seeking to be faithful to Christ. That *experience*—and the thoughtful and prayerful reflection on experience, interacting with Scripture—is an important aspect of a spiritual discernment process in the Ignatian model. It makes a big difference in my more general discernment about what I see the Father doing in the gay community.

What is God Doing in the Gay Community?

Before treating the question of gay marriage, I want to offer reflections on one other matter in light of the gay controversy. It is to ask a question that means a lot to me as a person of the Spirit, who believes that God is actively at work in the world *all the time*. The question is this: What is God doing in the gay community? What is the work of the Spirit among people who are gay and lesbian, as well as those who are transgender?

First, I must acknowledge that I'm not in the best position to answer this question. I must assume that the members of the gay community might best discern God's activity in the gay community. So the reader would be advised to take my thoughts on this matter as the confession of a pastor who has had too little understanding of this matter for too long.

Like so many in my generation, I first perceived the "gay community" as a subset of the larger category called "criminals" or "perverts." My earliest awareness of homosexuality came from hearing kids call other kids, "homo." I had to ask someone what that meant. I knew nothing of gay people from first-hand experience. I did know that the criminal code banned "sodomy."

The gay movement began when I was a teenager with the raid of a gay bar in New York City—a place where gay men hooked up anonymously in restrooms (since gay sex was criminalized). Who are homosexuals? All I knew was that they were men, many of them married, who have furtive sex in the bathrooms of gay bars and highway rest stops. In the 1980s this picture was reinforced by the outbreak of the AIDS epidemic, which we now know, took root in the gay bathhouses of San Francisco.

In *Culture of Desire: Paradox and Perversity in Gay Lives Today*, Frank Browning, a gay man and a reporter for NPR, describes the celebration of perversity that has been part of much gay culture. [144] This is exactly what one would expect from a culture driven underground by a dominant cultural view that sees all gay sex as inherently perverse. We see a similar embrace of negative stereotypes in other minority groups. But this is changing as gay people come out of the shadows.

As an evangelical pastor, I heard mainly about "the gay agenda" as another example of moral degradation, of encroaching, anti-Christian secularism. [145] But as I have come to know gay people though personal interactions, this negative impression isn't confirmed. The "gay community," like the "straight community" is a diverse community. And today we see many gay people who want to form lifelong unions, some in order to provide stable family units for children. I visit these couples in their homes and feel God's presence there as much as I do in any other family—which I do often when I

---

144 Browning, Frank. *Culture of Desire: Paradox and Perversity in Gay Lives Today*. New York, NY: Vintage Books, 1994.

145 John Stott, an evangelical whom I highly regard, in his commentary on Romans, chapter one, reflects this when he says, "The traditional interpretation, that they describe and condemns all homosexual behavior, is being challenged by the *gay lobby* [italics added]. Stott, John. *The Message of Romans: God's Good News for the World (Bible Speaks Today)*. Downers Grove, Ill.: IVP Academic, 2001, p. 77

enter homes. They have the same struggles and needs and they are seeking the same God for help.

My neighbors, Marissa and Judy, recently invited me over to meet their friends and watch the University of Michigan defeat Kansas in the NCAA tournament. They are parenting two children. Whatever anyone might think about them, I sense that they are a *family*. And it is difficult for me to imagine that God doesn't see them as a family as well. The phenomenon of such families who are living their lives openly is relatively new though. But only because they weren't allowed to live openly as families in the past.

Now I have a different discernment about what God is doing in "the gay community." I see a once-criminalized group of people, just coming out from living in the shadows, after centuries beneath a dark cloud of intense social shame and substantiated fears of physical violence. Yes, there are many in the gay community (as there are many straight people) who are deeply troubled. Living under such intense opprobrium isn't good for one's mental health. While the gay community was completely underground, a period that is not yet over, I don't know how many couples lived quietly and faithfully, perhaps going to church as "old maids living together." I'll bet there were plenty, but we'll never know since they were hidden from view.

Today, though, the "gay community" includes people I know and love who don't fit my negative stereotypes of an earlier time. Many of my fellow pastors have close family members who are gay. Some of these brothers, sisters, adult children, parents, would gladly commit to lifelong partnerships as an expression of their reverence for Christ, if there were churches that would have them.

Today we have gay people whose relationships, until just recently, have been branded by society as extraordinarily shameful, as uniquely perverse—worse than incest. The cultural heritage of this view had the effect of driving them all underground, where sex is practiced surreptitiously, secretively, for fear of social ostracism, not to mention physical harm. And now, tired of the highway rest stops, tired of the back rooms in gay bars, many in that community have a longing to attempt what can only be regarded as modern marvel regardless of gender: two people willing to attempt lifelong fidelity to each other, come what may.

This doesn't seem to me to be a "slippery slope." It seems to me that it might actually be instead, a redemptive trajectory. At least this is a possibility that we might thoughtfully consider, rather than something to resist at every turn.

"Could You See Yourself Performing a Gay Wedding?"

About five years ago, my wife Nancy and I had a pastor friend, Rich, and my literary agent, Kathryn, over for a day to talk about book publishing. Over dinner, we had a wide-ranging conversation about the gay issue. Nancy and I were quite candid about our growing concerns over the exclusionary policies of the church aimed at people in same-sex relationships.

At one point, Nancy went into a passionate oration on the subject, describing a lesbian couple she knew through her coaching activities. They were pregnant for the first time, looking for support, and were having trouble finding a church home. Rich asked Nancy point blank: "Could you see yourself performing a gay wedding?" Nancy didn't blink. She lifted up her head and said very calmly, "Yes. I think I could."

It reminded me very much of the time that we lay in bed together, nineteen years old, newly married, with an infant son in the other bedroom of our apartment in Married Student Housing at the University of Michigan. We had been exploring Christian faith together after years away from church— conversing with a Christian friend, reading the gospels for the first time, then *Mere Christianity* by C.S. Lewis. I had just written up a philosophical statement that traced my thinking about faith and how a person might come to the point of believing that Jesus revealed God to human beings. Nancy had just read my little treatise—about two pages on a yellow pad. She set the paper down in bed, looked up at me with that same calm look on her face and said, "Yes. I believe." I felt as though she had jumped off a cliff ahead of me.

It's now five years after Nancy answered Rich's question. How would I respond if Rich were to pose that same question to me today?

As posed, I'd answer it today as Nancy did then: I could see myself doing that. But "Could you see yourself performing a gay wedding?" calls for an imagined response to a future scenario in the abstract. The fact is, I've not been asked to perform such a ceremony yet. What if we sharpened the question from "Could you see yourself performing a gay wedding?" to the more categorical, "Would you perform a gay wedding?"

The fact is, I don't believe in giving a categorical answer to a question like this in the abstract. I tried that approach with the question of divorce and remarriage and found it wanting. Before any divorced person asked me to perform their wedding, I set out to decide, as a matter of policy, whether and when a remarriage was acceptable in the eyes of God. With experience, I discovered that my answer, developed in the abstract, was inadequate. This time, I plan to be open to the Spirit if a gay couple asks me to participate in a ceremony in which they pledge themselves to each other for life. To do that—to be led by the Spirit, that is—I imagine that I'll have to ignore the intense anxiety that surrounds pastors when the church and society are embroiled in the demonic throes of controversy.

That may seem naïve, but it's a studied naivety. Pastors operate in the realm of uncertainty much of the time. We are asked to make judgment calls that require the willingness to make one's best decision in particular circumstances. Every time we're asked to do a wedding for a divorced person, whether we know it or not, we are making such discernments.

When the morality of a given choice isn't settled within a community of faith, life doesn't pause until the matter is settled. This is a normal and unavoidable part of life in the community of Jesus followers. We currently have plenty of issues like this. We've granted the gay issue a special status as somehow more significant than all these other unresolved moral questions. We subject decisions about *this* issue to intense scrutiny. Why? Because it has become our controversy *de jour*. But life happens whether or not we've settled *all* these questions and people make choices and pastors are invited into the mix to offer their counsel, presence, prayers, and deeds. If that's an unsettling or frightening prospect, pity the poor pastor.

If you are a pastor, you better have your wits about you when your care for someone, especially someone in a position of great vulnerability, draws you into the orbit of a controversy. Do you let the fires of controversy shape your response? Or do you give your full attention to the person before you, as though they were the sheep of his pasture, and you his under-shepherd? You better put your focus on the latter and let the former take care of itself.

In the meantime, this question has gotten me thinking about what it means to participate as a pastor in a wedding, any wedding.

These are my thoughts as I consider that question.

I don't view marriage as a sacrament as some do. [146] The sacraments of baptism and communion, the two recognized by the churches of the Protestant Reformation, are linked to the life of the age to come—the New Creation, the concern of the gospel—in a way that marriage is not. [147] Good call,

---

146 Roman Catholicism, Anglicanism, and Eastern Orthodoxy recognize seven sacraments (including marriage). The churches of the Protestant Reformation generally recognize two: baptism and communion.

147 Baptism is related to new creation because it signals a new birth into the new creation. Communion is related to new creation because

Protestant Reformers. But whether marriage is viewed as a
sacrament or not, the pastors, priests, or leaders who preside
at the weddings are not making the marriage happen. The
two people who have decided to cast their lot with each
other are doing that. Even in Catholic sacramental theology,
which normally reserves a privileged role for the priest in
the performance of the sacraments, it is clear that the couple
themselves perform the sacrament, not the priest. (For this
reason, it's the only sacrament in Catholic understanding that
can be performed by a woman.) It makes me wonder: does the
common practice of a pastor pronouncing a couple husband
and wife (in the name of the State and the gospel) obscure this
fact? Does the couple own their decision to marry a little less
if they think marriage is something someone else effects by
solemn words? Would it be better, especially in the trenches of
married life to remember: *we did this, we effected this, because
we freely decided to.* Maybe it would be truer to the reality if
the pastor simply offered prayers for the couple.

To date, all the marriages that I have participated in as
pastor have been state-sanctioned. I have been operating
as a duly authorized agent of the State of Michigan, signing
a marriage license provided by the State of Michigan.
Marriage is denied gay couples in the State of Michigan by
constitutional amendment. So I won't be doing any such
weddings as an agent of the State anytime soon, unless the
constitution is amended again or the Supreme Court rules
such restrictions unconstitutional.

But someone, probably someone I know and love, maybe
two moms with a son or daughter depending on them for
care, protection, love, guidance, comfort, and stability, might
ask me to participate with them in a ceremony in which they
express their commitment to each other and invite God to be
the center of their relationship. When they do, I won't take it

---

it anticipates the coming banquet feast to be celebrated when the new
creation arrives in fullness. Marriage is for this age, not the age to
come.

lightly. I'll talk with them, pray, discern, and seek to do what seems good, to me and to the Holy Spirit. Then, if I'm half the pastor I want to be, I'll do that.

As this historic issue regarding marriage is sorted out, we have breathing room, though, to hold to our convictions on this matter and to respect the dictates of our own conscience. We don't have to approve of each other's decisions regarding whom to marry in order to be in community with each other. It just means that we have to accept each other for the sake of Christ. We have to agree not to judge each other over these decisions, not to separate from each other as if our staying in relationship amounts to some kind of moral approval. The fact is, the gospel empowers us to be in relationship with each other despite our moral disapproval over any number of concerns.

If we want it. If we are willing to live by it.

CHAPTER 7

I Am Willing

THE FACT THAT I invested a lot of prayer in this discernment process by no means guarantees the validity of its conclusions. But I am writing as your pastor and I'd like to reveal a little more about the *spiritual* struggle that I've been through in the process of arriving at these conclusions. Even now, I'm tempted to look back and think, "What was the big deal? Isn't this all plain to see?" I only wish it had been!

Years from now, when all the anxiety in church and society has moved on to some other issue, I suspect we'll have a hard time understanding what the big deal was. Already, many young Jesus followers wonder what all the angst is about. But this is not years from now. The tough issues that a pastor deals with, especially these conflict-laden controversial ones, are difficult because they hit us in the deepest part of our being, where honest engagement with God happens.

You can't get to a place of clarity without engaging in a kind of wrestling prayer that takes you into territory (in your own psyche) that you wouldn't otherwise dare to stumble through. How does a pastor share that sort of thing with his congregation? What I have written so far doesn't begin to do it justice.

I didn't think I could, until I stumbled upon this list of statements taped into the back page of my copy of *The Divine Hours*, written at the end of a five-day silent retreat several years ago. [148] I was in the throes of rethinking my position on the gay issue at this time. Reading the statements several years later, as I happened to while I was preparing this letter for you, made me realize how important my experience of God has been in shaping my perspective. Or what I believe to have been my experience of God.

I don't say that to claim divine authority for anything I've written here. I say it by way of confession. Maybe if I just tell you what I can, I might be better understood by you, the congregation I serve as pastor. Like God, we all want to be understood.

This is what I wrote:

I am willing....

> *To go wherever it is these treasures are from*
> *To be led by the fire of divine love*
> *To offend the tribal phantom projected from below*
> *over evangelicalism*
> *To seek and save what is lost*
> *To become docile and receptive to the advances of*
> *the Holy Spirit*
> *To learn how to sing the Song of Songs*
> *To be the Lord's handmaiden*
> *To be misunderstood*
> *To be fearless*
> *To be wrong again*
> *To continue*

---

148 The retreat was part of my internship in Ignatian spirituality in 2006. We had an assignment to write down a personal "Credo" statement drawn from the reflection that occurred over the course of the silent retreat.

See what I mean? To disclose these statements is a little embarrassing. A friend who read this section called it, "a little mushy." Yep. Those middle ones about being docile and receptive to the advances of the Spirit, learning how to sing the Song of Songs, and the handmaiden bit, especially—if not mushy, oddly romantic, perhaps?

I'll just forge ahead and offer my reflections on what these statements mean to me.

First, notice the language. It's dramatic, one might even say melodramatic. *I am willing … to go wherever it is these treasures are from, blah, blah, blah. Please!!*

I have learned that there's no way to open yourself to the experience of God while retaining your cool, your sense of ironic detachment. Life with this God, apparently, is a drama—part tragedy, part comedy, part fairy tale [149] —but it is nothing like the chatty dialogue of, say, *The West Wing*, my favorite show of all time.

I am willing…to go wherever it is these treasures are from.

Around the time of this retreat, I was in a period of what in the Ignatian tradition would be called an intense and extended time of "consolation." Meaning I was experiencing more of the comfort, consolation, and stupefying goodness of God than I thought was possible for one human being—especially one who is wired as I am—to enjoy. It didn't last forever. I knew that it couldn't, meaning I knew that I couldn't handle it, but I also knew that I was in something real and something special that I didn't want to shy away from. And, somehow, I knew— and here I can't say anything more because I only know this intuitively—that my willingness to rethink "the gay issue" was part of the price to be paid for what I was experiencing.

---

149 From my favorite book on preaching, *The Gospel as Tragedy, Comedy, and Fairy Tale*, by Frederick Buechner.

Wherever it is.

That's a kind of ruthless thing to say. I have felt that I've needed to be a little bit ruthless in pursuit of this. As in "forge ahead, come what may." In one of these prayer times that I mentioned in my period of extended consolation, I found myself rolling around on the floor, ah, screaming. I was in this state because I had seen a vision (and I don't have these things often, so infrequent as to be *memorable*) of a gate opening in the middle of a crowd and the crowd was screaming, like people getting crushed at one of those soccer match tragedies. Only I knew that the one opening the gate was the Son of Man, and nothing was going to stop him opening it. As happens sometimes when he opens the gates of the kingdom to people who otherwise hadn't gained admittance before.

I am willing … to be led by the fire of divine love.

During this period of intense and extended consolation, I was surprised one morning to be inexorably lowered from my mind, somewhere into my heart, in which there was a cave. And sitting there, as if on a log in the cave, was a figure I took to be Jesus. No, it was Jesus, if I know anything of Jesus at all. So I sat down next to him—I'm not sure there's any point in looking straight at him, at least not for me in my current state—and together we found ourselves staring into a fire. I've since come to regard that fire as the fire of divine love. What else would Jesus be staring into?

I have written about this experience in *Mystically Wired*, and mentioned it a time or two in sermons. But not all of it. Not one of the most sensitive parts of it.

To keep the experience going—whatever this was, I didn't want it to end, ever—I started to mention by name different people that I knew. Just mentioning each name in the hearing of the one sitting next to me as we looked into the fire. I went down my usual prayer list, and when that was done I added a few names. Including the name of a sister of Julie who was on my list. And when I said, "Julie's sister" and then added the fact that she had a child, he said, "And another one's on the way." Which I took hold of in my mind because it was a data point for the real world. Later that day, I went to Julie's husband, Don, and said, "Is Julie's sister pregnant by any chance?" And Don said, "Yes, just newly. Nobody knows yet. How did you know that?"

This only served to frighten, not console me, because it made me feel that perhaps I had been sitting next to the dear Lord Jesus, and I wasn't sure how I felt about that. Strange. The thing one thinks one longs for happens, and you feel all mixed up inside. What's up with that?

But what I haven't mentioned, except to a few people, is this: one of the people whose name I brought up while I was staring into that fire was "Phyllis Tickle." When I did, I shot out of the cave with a startled fright. Things were murky after that for a minute, but I decided to go back to the cave for a proper exit and I did.

For the longest time, that bothered me. What was that all about? Here's what I think, after years of reflection. I had become friends with Phyllis Tickle when I asked if we might load her compilation of prayers called *The Divine Hours*™ on our church website. And surprisingly, she and her publisher said, "Sure." After which we began to correspond by email from time to time, and eventually Phyllis invited me and Nancy and our daughter Grace to visit with her and her husband Sam at their home in Lucy, Tenn.

Somewhere in this time frame, I invited Phyllis to come to speak at the Vineyard Church of Ann Arbor. Before she agreed to come, Phyllis said, "There's something you should know about me first, Ken. I don't want to blindside you. The pastor at the church Sam and I are attending is gay." I think I said something calm and collected like, "Phyllis!!! The gay issue is radioactive!!! You know that, don't you???" To which she said something like, "I know." And then I summoned my best self and said, "Why should that make any difference? We'd love to have you."

At the time of my experience in the cave, sitting with Jesus around a fire, I associated Phyllis with "the gay issue." I think that when I mentioned Phyllis Tickle in the cave and shot out immediately from the most tender and vivid experience that I have ever had of the dear Lord Jesus, it was fear of the gay issue that surfaced in my heart and shot me out of the cave.

I was sitting next to Jesus in that cave, and his perfect love was casting out fear. I left with it because I was holding onto it.

In the Ignatian discernment process, there's something called "discernment of spirits." The gist of it is this: when a person is moving toward God, the "good spirit" is experienced as consoling, comforting, soothing, while the "bad spirit" is experienced as alarming, frightening, disturbing. When a person is moving away from God, it's the exact opposite.

In the cave, I think I was moving toward God, and the spirit that alarmed, frightened and disturbed me was the bad spirit, not the good one.

This has given me some way to measure just how potent is the fear around "the gay issue" for someone like me, a pastor in a church within the orbit of American evangelicalism. To think that something like that had the power to disturb me when I was sitting in what seemed to me to be the closest possible proximity to the dear Lord Jesus, desire of the everlasting hills and my own heart! Only the most intense and powerful fear could have had that effect on me in that setting.

I am willing…to offend the phantom projected from below over evangelicalism.

The image that informed this statement was from one of the Batman movies, where the Batman bat appears in the night clouds projected from below, over Gotham city. I don't even know who in the movie projects the image—Batman, his helper, or someone else? All I know is that things can appear over us to be larger or more imposing than they really are and that such things can be projected from below.

During the retreat, I must have been coming to grips with this in order to write down such a statement. Now it's as plain to me as the nose on my face, if that's my nose in the mirror, that is. Religious systems, even good ones, have things from below that get projected over them or even through them. These things serve to impose their will over the people affected by them.

I have come to see the sheer size, scope, and intensity of the "gay controversy" as it has affected American evangelicalism in this light, or rather, under this shadow obscuring the light. I think the controversy itself is a phantom projected from below over American evangelicalism. Knowing this, I don't think we should give it the credence or the pride of place that it wants. We should see it as something much smaller than it appears. Psychologically, I don't think I would have been capable of engaging this issue with any other approach. It's been hard enough as it is holding to that perspective.

So I guess I couldn't proceed if I weren't willing to offend whatever this is.

I don't think we should be eager to offend anything or anyone. But sometimes in order to walk faithfully with Jesus, we have to be *willing* to offend some things.

Obviously, this has informed my approach to this question. Everything around us screams, "This is a huge issue! This is the defining issue of our times!" But I think that's only the phantom of fear speaking. There are much bigger moral issues than this one to attend to. Surely the kingdom of God would be better served if we were to invest our moral energy into discerning what we're to do about greed, war-making, gossip, to name a few.

When I presented my paper at the Society of Vineyard Scholars, the place was packed. I think there may have been more people in the room than signed up for the conference. Or maybe that was just my nerves estimating crowd size. It seemed that people in the room were super alert, despite the late afternoon hour. After I was done presenting, a long line of people queued up and the moderator of the session extended the Q & A time to deal with all the questions.

By contrast, my fellow Vineyard pastor, Jason Clark from the U.K., a real scholar, gave a paper on the relationship between the evangelical movement and capitalism in the United States and the United Kingdom. Jason has done his dissertation work on this topic, so he's thought long and hard and deep about it, and he's done so as a pastor. He's done some terrific work helping the people in his church grapple with the economic pressures we're all under in our particular economic system. If ever there were a pastor you wanted to listen to about a compelling moral issue of our time—greed—Jason would be the person to hear out. Yet, the room was packed for my paper and there were only a scattering of people in the room for his.

Afterward, I joked with him that the disparity in crowd size for our respective papers was an indication of the displaced moral concern within our religious tribe for the topic of my paper, a concern that would be more proportionate were it given to the topic of his paper. I feel that I'm not betraying a confidence to say that he agreed with me.

When I shared my growing concerns about this issue with Berten Waggoner, then the National Director of the Vineyard USA, he said something I'll never forget: "Ken, if you choose to speak out on this topic, your work as a pastor will be forever defined by this issue. Are you willing to do that?" I guess so. But why would such a thing be so? There are many things I've devoted myself to with much greater energy than this thing. Like teaching from the Bible many hundreds of Sundays on many hundreds of topics other than this.

I am willing…to seek and save what is lost.

In this letter, I've mentioned the missionary concern associated with this question. In a place like Ann Arbor, the burden of proof shifts from "When in doubt, continue the traditional exclusion" to "When in doubt, place the traditional exclusion under greater scrutiny." I have placed the traditional exclusionary practice under greater scrutiny and found it wanting.

But I want to insist: I have taken this approach in my role as a *pastor*, more than in my role as a missionary. Jesus was a pastor. His word for it was "shepherd." (A pastor is really just a sheep dog working for the Great Shepherd.) As a good shepherd, Jesus had an eye out for the lost sheep. When we lose sight of that, I think we've lost sight of what it means to be a pastor, something we pastors do often.

> *I am willing ... to become docile and receptive to*
> *the advances of the Holy Spirit*
> *to learn how to sing the Song of Songs*
> *to be the Lord's handmaiden*

These are the statements I feel shy about including. Partly because to this day I'm not sure what they mean. Obviously, they have something to do with gender and sexuality, but in a way that is trying for a pastor of my generation to comprehend, let alone discuss. But maybe that's the blessing of age. You loosen up a little.

On the retreat, I do know that God was dealing with me very personally and in a way that seemed connected to my gender and sexuality. I did a meditation on Genesis 2, where Adam is put to sleep and God brings Eve out of his side. It turned into an unexpected meditation in which I was Adam upon awaking, to find my wife Nancy as Eve by my side. And I just took my time walking around her, the two of us naked in God's presence, looking at each other.

Which, I will admit, I'm a little uncomfortable mentioning.

But how far from the glory of God are we in our discomfort with our own sexuality!? And how at ease, by contrast, is God with a creation that is as frankly sexual as the one he breathed into being? Maybe that's what learning "how to sing the Song of Songs" was all about?

And I do know that on the retreat, God came close to me, as I pondered a painting of Mary that was in my Catholic retreat center room. Jesus had a mom he was close to and that person was a woman.

Through that, perhaps, I was being invited to consider the value of some things that are, rightly or wrongly, traditionally associated with femininity more than masculinity. To follow Jesus, women are called to do some things that are traditionally associated with masculinity rather than femininity: be bold, assertive, onward Christian soldiers and all that. [150] We're all—male and female—called sons of God. And we're all—male and female—part of the bride of Christ. Maybe we are being asked to relax around gender distinctions a little.

But more to the point: part of the reason the church is so conflicted about matters of sexuality is that people in churches, including pastors, are conflicted about matters of sexuality. If not conflicted, then "not at ease with." Sexuality is everyone's tender territory. In the same way that we have difficulty talking about our experience of God, we have difficulty talking about our sexuality. Which means we have difficulty thinking honestly about it. Pastors no less than anyone else.

And this has made it very difficult for us to handle an issue like this with more care, candor, honesty, courage, and gentleness. Which, in turn, has made it very difficult for people who are deeply affected by these things to find a home with God in the church.

I am willing...to be misunderstood.

150 The Bible, of course, blows some of our traditional gender categorizations out of the water. Deborah and Judith come to mind as women who seemed to be nothing like the gender stereotypes associated with femininity! Isn't the Bible wonderful?

Maybe this is just part of the cost of being human. To be human is to speak, as God spoke. Every time we speak, we become vulnerable to being misunderstood. In order to speak, we have to be willing to be misunderstood.

I hate it when people misunderstand me. I say one thing, and people hear another. Ah! And as Nancy pointed out from time to time, sometimes I don't make it easy for people.

One of her most cogent sermon critiques went like this: "If that's what you meant, I can guarantee you that's not what many people heard." And then I would search for what cannot be found: the rewind button.

But that's part of what keeps everyone mum when there's a phantom projected from below over your religious community: we don't want to say anything for fear of being misunderstood. The only solution is to show an unreasonable regard for the ability of others to listen well, to hear your heart even if your words are muddled.

I am willing...to be fearless.

Of course, I'm not fearless. I'm riddled with fear, because as a human being, I am the offspring of a long line of people with an overactive alarm system, necessary for survival in a hostile world. In fact, all of my direct ancestors, like yours, survived long enough to breed, precisely because their alarm system didn't fail them. The only way out of the fear that comes with an overactive alarm system is the willingness to pretend to be fearless, just as the only way out of sadness sometimes is the willingness to pretend to be sad less.

When I presented this as a paper at the Society of Vineyard Scholars, a number of people, including the respondent who didn't agree with my conclusions, commented on my "courage" in presenting the paper. At first, this appealed to my natural desire to look good. But after hearing it several times, that wore off and it gave way to anger.

I thought of the believers I know in a nation I don't even want to mention in print because they wake up in small villages that have been affected by a militant form of Islam and have to decide whether to be known as Jesus followers or not. That takes courage.

And then I thought of the people who are gay or transgender who now attend the Vineyard Church of Ann Arbor, knowing just a little of the fear that they went through simply to attend a church not knowing whether they would be accepted or not. That takes courage.

But I had to admit, giving the paper at the Society of Vineyard Scholars took a little moxie, a little *chutzpah*, a little nerve. Maybe, if the bar is very low, it took a little courage. But then, what does that say about the religious system that we are operating in? That it takes a little *courage* for a pastor to stand up and talk about things that every pastor faces when it comes to the care of people who are gay, lesbian and transgender? Shouldn't that take any number of things other than courage? Why would such a word have any use at all in such a context?

We should all be ashamed to admit that it takes any courage at all for a pastor to do such a thing.

I am willing … to be wrong again.

Of the statements I wrote down at that silent retreat, this is the one that almost didn't make the cut.

A little background might help. I came to faith as a young adult in the context of a period of intense spiritual renewal (the Jesus movement, and then the charismatic renewal) populated by young, intense, baby-boomers who felt they were on a mission from God to change the world and didn't need much help from anyone else. We were up for intense spiritual experience and we got it. I have since come to wonder if, when the Spirit comes to such an eager human being, the entirety of that human being—good, bad, beautiful, and ugly—is intensified, is animated.

Many of us were leaders at a young age in movements brimming over with more zeal than wisdom. I made some mistakes with big consequences, and I have lived long enough to notice and deeply regret them. It's a profoundly humbling experience at best, with plenty of self-imposed humiliation thrown in for extra measure.

I have in mind a searing experience about twenty-five years ago, when the other leaders in a renewalist Christian community selected me to speak publically about some of the significant leadership mistakes we had made over the years. I spoke before two thousand people, with press in attendance judging by the article that showed up in the local paper soon afterward. The decision to make this presentation put one group of leaders in the local group at odds with another group of leaders in another group, and the whole thing turned into a big mess that led to a great unraveling.

They say disillusionment is a huge step in a person's spiritual growth, especially when it involves disillusionment with a false view of one's self as someone who doesn't make big mistakes.

We so want to be right and so trust that our desire to be right is something that God would surely bless. Yet the desire to be right comes with a price: the fear of being wrong. And so, in a counter-intuitive way, this focus on being right seems to be the porridge we settle for when we exchange our birthright because we're famished and fear that father won't feed us.

It's what I worried about before I met Jesus: I so wanted and needed to be right. It was up to me to figure out what that meant. I was alone in the universe yet my experience of the universe suggested that I was expected to be right. I tried, but found it existentially exhausting.

And then I met Jesus. And he seemed to be so good, so true, so pure, so admirable, so full of, as Jonathan Edwards loved to say, excellency. Right paled in comparison to all that.

But it is an addiction, especially in the realm of religion, and I've gone back to it to many times.

Or something like this seemed to be what God was dealing with on that retreat. Not my godly caution, my fear of offending him. But my ungodly caution, my fear of being wrong—the thing that keeps more people from following Jesus than perhaps any other thing.

Perhaps you can appreciate the obvious: any pastor within the orbit of American evangelicalism might understandably be subject to an intense fear of being wrong over this issue. You may think of me as a confident pastor, and I have plenty of confidence I suppose. But don't think I haven't also experienced some deep anguish about the possibility of being wrong. It's just that I felt moved by the Spirit not to give way to that fear, because I have been led to believe that it is not part of the new creation happening in me.

Let me just take a moment to state the obvious, for my benefit as much as for yours: I have been wrong before as a pastor. I have written at least one book that I refused to allow back into print because the publisher wouldn't allow me to revise it. I can appreciate anyone disagreeing me because I have lived long enough—it took a while—to disagree with myself.

I might be wrong again and I might be wrong on this matter. But I am determined not to let the fear of that keep me from following Jesus as I understand him to be leading me.

Which is why

I am willing…to continue.

References

Blankenhorn, David. *The Future of Marriage*. New York, N.Y.: Encounter Books, 2007.

Bonhoeffer, Dietrich. *Ethics*. New York, N.Y.: The MacMillan Co., 1965. pp. 17-20.

Boswell, John. *Christianity, Social Tolerance, and Homosexuality: Gay People in Western Europe from the Beginning of the Christian Era to the Fourteenth Century*. Chicago and London: The University of Chicago Press, 1980.

Bromley, Don. *The One Ultimate Ethic: A Critique of William Webbs "Slaves Women, and Homosexuals"*. Society of Vineyard Scholars Annual Conference, 2011.

Brooten, Bernadette. "Patristic Interpretations of Romans 1:26." *Studia Patristica XVIII: Papers of the 1983 Oxford Patristics Conference*. Ed. Elizabeth Livingstone.(1985): 338-340. The Writings of St. Paul: Annotated Texts, Reception and Criticism. 2d ed. vol. 1 Ed. Wayne A. Meeks and John T. Fitzgerald. New York: Norton, 2007. pp. 287-288.

Browning, Frank. *Culture of Desire: Paradox and Perversity in Gay Lives Today*. New York, N.Y.: Vintage Books, 1994.

Buechener, Frederick. *Telling the Truth: The Gospel as Tragedy, Comedy, and Fairy Tale*. New York, N.Y.: HarperOne, 2009.

Buxton, Richard. *The Complete World of Greek Mythology*. New York, N.Y.: Thames and Hudson, 2004.

Callahan, Gerald N. *Between XX and XY: Intersexuality and the Myth of Two Sexes*. Chicago, Ill: Chicago Review Press, 2009.

Cantarella, Eva. *Bisexuality in the Ancient World*. New Haven and London: Yale University Press, 2002.

Clapp, Steve., Leverton Helbert, Kristen., and Zizak Angela. *Faith Matters: Teenagers, Religion & Sexuality (LifeQuest Growing in Faith Series)*. Bellevue, Wash.: LifeQuest, 2003.

D. Martyn-Lloyd Jones. *Romans: Exposition of Chapter 14: 1-17, Liberty and Conscience*. East Peoria, Ill.: Versa Press, 2011.

Dunn, James. D. G. *Word Biblical Commentary: Volume 38A, Romans 1-8*. Nashville, Tenn.: Thomas Nelson, 1988.

Eckholm, Eric. *Rift Forms in Movement as Belief in Gay 'Cure' Is Renounced*. New York Times, July 2012.

Fee, Gordon. D. *The First Epistle to the Corinthians, The New International Commentary on the New Testament*. Grand Rapids, Mich.: William B. Eerdmans Publishing Co., 1987.

Fitzmyer, Joseph A. *Romans: The Anchor Yale Bible Commentaries*. New Haven, Conn.: Yale University Press, 1993.

Gagnon, Robert A. J. *The Bible and Homosexual Practice*. Nashville, Tenn.; Abingdon Press, 2001.

Gallagher, Timothy. *Discerning the Will of God*. New York, N.Y.: The Crossroad Publishing Co., 2009.

Gates, Gary J. *How many people are lesbian, gay, bisexual and transgender?* The Williams Institute, University of California School of Law, April 2001.

Gottman, John and Silver, Nan. *The Seven Principles for Making Marriage Work*. New York, N.Y.: Three Rivers Press, 1999.

Haidt, Jonathan. *The Righteous Mind: Why Good People Are Divided by Politics and Religion*. New York, N.Y.: Pantheon Books, 2012.

Hatzenbuehler, Mark L.; McLaughlin, Katie A; Keyes, Katherine M. and Hasin, Deborah S. *The Impact of Institutional Discrimination on Psychiatric Disorders in Lesbian, Gay, and Bisexual Populations: A Prospective Study. American*

Journal of Public Health: March 2010, Vol. 100, No. 3, pp. 452-459.

Hays, Richard. B. *The Moral Vision of The New Testament, A Contemporary Introduction to New Testament Ethics*. New York, N.Y.: HarperCollins, 1996.

Hill, Wesley and Greene McCreight, Kathryn. *Washed and Waiting: Reflections on Christian Faithfulness and Homosexuality*. Grand Rapids, Mich.: Zondervan, 2012.

Jewett, Paul. *Christian Tolerance, Paul's Message to the Modern Church*. Philadelphia, Pa.: The Westminster Press, 1982.

Jewett, Robert. *Romans: A Commentary*. Minneapolis, Minn.: Fortress Press, 2007.

Johnson Luke Timothy. *Reading Romans: A Literary and Theological Commentary*. Macon, Ga.: Smyth and Helwys, 2012.

Jung, Patricia Beattie. *Heterosexism: An Ethical Challenge*. Albany, N.Y.: State University of New York Press, 1993.

Kelley, Dean M. *Why Conservative Churches are Growing: A Study in Sociology of Religion*. New York, N.Y.: Harper & Row, Publishers, 1972.

Klawans, Jonathan. *Impurity and Sin in Ancient Judaism* Oxford, United Kingdom: Oxford University Press, 2000.

Lee, Justin. *Torn: Rescuing the Gospel from the Gay vs. Christians Debate*. New York, N.Y.: Jericho Books, 2012.

Longo, Joseph, N.; Walls, and Wisneski, Hope. *Religion and religiosity: protective or harmful factors for sexual minority youth? Mental Health, Religion & Culture*, 2013 Vol. 16, No. 3, pp. 273-290.

Marin, Andrew. *Love is an Orientation*. Downers Grove, Ill.: InterVarsity Press, 2009.

Moo, Douglas J. *The Epistle to the Romans, The New International Commentary on the New Testament*. Grand Rapids, Mich.: Eerdmans, 1996.

Nathan, Rich and Wilson, Ken. *Empowered Evangelicals*. Boise, Idaho: Ampelon Publishing, 2009.

Ngak, Chenda. *Facebook releases map of marriage equality support*. CBS News, March 29, 2013.

Olsen, Roger E. *The Mosaic of Christian Belief: Twenty Centuries of Unity and Diversity*. Downer's Grove, Ill.: Inter Varsity Press, 2002.

Oppenheimer, Mark. *In Shift, an Activist Enlists Same-Sex Couples in a Pro-Marriage Coalition*. New York Times, January 29, 2013.

Osborne, Grant. R. *Romans (IVP New Testament Commentary)* Downers Grove, Ill,: IVP Academic, 2010.

Philo, *The Special Laws*, III, VII, 40-42 (40).

Putnam, Robert. D and Campbell, David. E. *American Grace: How Religion Divides Us*. New York, N.Y.: Simon & Schuster, 2010.

Reasoner, Mark. *The Strong and the Weak: Romans 14:1-15:13 in Context*. Cambridge, United Kingdom: Cambridge University Press, 1999.

Rodgers, Jack. *Jesus, The Bible, and Homosexuality; Explode the Myths, Heal the Church*. Louisville, Ky.: Westminster John Knox Press, 2006.

Ruden, Sarah. *Paul Among the People*. New York, N.Y.: Random House Inc., 2008.

Sampley, Paul. J.; Wall, Robert. W.; Wright, N.T. *The New Interpreter's Bible : Acts - First Corinthians: Volume 10*. Nashville, Tenn.: Abingdon Press, 2002.

Soards, Marion. L. *Scripture and Homosexuality, Biblical Authority and the Church Today*. Louisville, Ky.: Westminster John Knox Press, 1995.

Stott, John. *The Message of Romans: God's Good News for the World (Bible Speaks Today)*. Downers Grove, Ill,: IVP Academic, 2001.

Switzer, David K. *Pastoral Care of Gays, Lesbians and Their Families*. Minneapolis, Minn.: Augsburg Fortress, 1999.

Taussig, Hal. *In the Beginning was the Meal*. Minneapolis, Minn.: Fortress Press, 2009.

Vatican II (The Second Vatican Council) *Pastoral Constitution on the Church in the Modern World Gaudium et spes*, Promulgated by His Holiness, Pope Paul VI, December 7, 1965.

Via, Dan O. and Gagnon, Robert, A. J. *Homosexuality and the Bible: Two Views*. Minneapolis, Minn.: Fortress Press, 2003.

Volf, Miroslav. *Exclusion and Embrace: A Theological Exploration of Identity, Otherness and Reconciliation*. Nashville, Tenn.: Abingdon Press, 1996.

Wilson, Glenn and Rahman, Qazi. *Born Gay: The Psychobiology of Sex Orientation*. London, United Kingdom: Peter Owen Ltd, 2008.

Wilson, Ken. *Mystically Wired: Exploring New Realms in Prayer*. Nashville, Tenn.: Thomas Nelson, 2010.

Wright, N. T. *The New Interpreter's Bible: Acts - 1 Corinthians: Volume 10*. Nashville, Tenn.: Abingdon Press, 2002.

Wright, N. T. *Communion and Koinonia: Pauline Reflections on Tolerance and Boundaries*. A paper given at the *Future of Anglicanism Conference*, Oxford, 2002.

Acknowledgements

MY THANKS TO my adult children, Jesse (and Veronica), Maja, Amy (and Ben), Judy (and Mike), and Grace, who have affected me as much as I, them, and have kept my mind and heart open. And to my sisters, Marilyn and Nancy, who patiently bore the curiosities of a brother affected by earnest, renewalist faith.

To the Read the Spirit team: John Hile, David Crumm, Becky Hile, Rick Nease, Henry Passenger and Kelly Hughes. I needed an innovative publisher I could trust and I got it.

And to so many others who have been conversation partners along the way.

Rick Rykowski, my dearest friend. And Bill Elkington, my brother-in-law. To James Rhodenhiser and Levon. To Andrew Marin. To Don Postema, my spiritual director, who one day suggested I ask Jesus what he thought about all this. To Gordon Prepsky who cured my claustrophobia. To my pastoral colleagues on the Vineyard Church of Ann Arbor staff who spent countless hours thinking, talking, exploring, agreeing, disagreeing, discerning: Donnell Wyche, Don Bromley, Emily Swan, Diane Sonda, Shaun Garth Walker, Nigel Berry, Penny Johnson, Jamie Bott, Shonagh Chimbira (the latter worked closely with me in the preparation of the manuscript and served as first reader and research assistant.) Special thanks to Donnell for his role in keeping the church working while I mourned the sudden loss of my wife, Nancy, who was my key partner in this work of discernment.

My thanks to the sixty lay leaders in our church who read this manuscript first and poked and prodded and encouraged me along the way. For the congregation that loved me through loss, becoming my church home in ways I hadn't realized I needed. Especially those who first read this (long) letter when I made it available on request, about 200 in all, many of whom offered feedback along the way. To my two small groups with whom I processed much of this: Kirk, Rick, Dana, Glen and Bob, Derek, Paul, Mike, Brad. To our church board, Mary Ann, Glen, Steve, Chris, Andrea, Jake. To my national director (now retired) Berten Waggoner, the most theologically adept pastor I know. To the many pastors in my tribe, Vineyard, who disagreed with my conclusions but did so with love and grace. And to Dave, Charles, Brian, Steve, Adey, Lucas, Christina and Kristina. To Dick Bieber who called me recently.

To Phyllis Tickle, wife of Dr. Sam Tickle, to whom this work is dedicated.

And to Julia and her daughter, Oceana.

Most of all, to the unnamed gay, lesbian and transgender people whose lives have revealed Jesus to me.

About the Author

Photo by Ernesto Medina

KEN WILSON IS founding pastor of Vineyard Church of Ann Arbor, a multi-cultural congregation. He is known nationwide for his work in evangelical environmental initiatives and fostering contemplative prayer. Ken is author of *Empowered Evangelicals* (with Rich Nathan), *Jesus Brand Spirituality*, and, most recently, *Mystically Wired*.

Colophon

READ THE SPIRIT Books produces its titles using innovative digital systems that serve the emerging wave of readers who want their books delivered in a wide range of formats—from traditional print to digital readers in many shapes and sizes. This book was produced using this entirely digital process that separates the core content of the book from details of final presentation, a process that increases the flexibility and accessibility of the book's text and images. At the same time, our system ensures a well-designed, easy-to-read experience on all reading platforms, built into the digital data file itself.

David Crumm Media has built a unique production workflow employing a number of XML (Extensible Markup Language) technologies. This workflow allows us to create a single digital "book" data file that can be delivered quickly in all formats from traditionally bound print-on-paper to nearly any digital reader you care to choose, including Amazon Kindle®, Apple iBook®, Barnes and Noble Nook® and other devices that support the ePub and PDF digital book formats.

And due to the efficient "print-on-demand" process we use for printed books, we invite you to visit us online to learn more about opportunities to order quantities of this book with the possibility of personalizing a "group read" for your organization or congregation by putting your organization's logo and name on the cover of the copies you order. You can even add your own introductory pages to this book for your church or organization.

During production, we use Adobe InDesign®, <Oxygen/>® XML Editor and Microsoft Word® along with custom tools built in-house.

The print edition is set in Minion Pro and Myriad Pro.

Cover art and Design by Rick Nease: www.RickNeaseArt.com.

Content editing by David Crumm.

Copy editing and XML styling by Henry Passenger.

Digital encoding and print layout by John Hile.

If you enjoyed this book, you may also enjoy

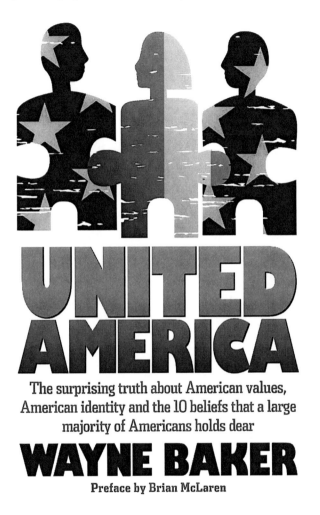

UNITED AMERICA

The surprising truth about American values,
American identity and the 10 beliefs that a large
majority of Americans holds dear

WAYNE BAKER

Preface by Brian McLaren

Sociologist Dr. Wayne Baker reports that Americans are united by 10 Core Values that are strongly held by a majority of Americans, are stable over time and are shared across diverse demographic, religious and political lines.

http://UnitedAmericaBook.com

ISBN: 978-1-939880-05-5

If you enjoyed this book, you may also enjoy

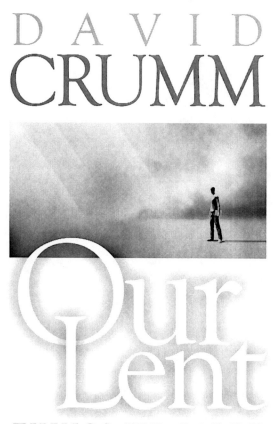

DAVID CRUMM

Our Lent

THINGS WE CARRY

"Our Lent" is a 40-chapter journey with Jesus, written by award-winning Religion Writer David Crumm, that pauses each day to explore the enduring power of the things Jesus showed us, many of them quite tangible.

http://www.OurLent.com

ISBN: 978-1934879-016